7 STAGES OF ONE SIDED LOVE

SIDDHANTH RAWAT

To my schoolmates

Contents

Acknowledgements

This book would not have been possible without many
people, From my seniors to my teachers and even my
peers and also some of my juniors, everyone is involved in
some way shape or form
Special thanks to a few of my friends and teachers
For the support and love while writing the book

Preface

Dear Reader,

Have you ever been in one-sided love?, Well, it causes some pain to know that the one you love so much that you are willing to sacrifice your life for her/him, But that person does not even have feelings for you.

Well, I know that pain and so at such a tender age of 15. Well, it is said that When Cupid flies in the wrong direction, shoots the arrow without looking and hits the wrong person, One-sided love begins,

It is definitely the most painful kind of love and may even be the first kind of love for many, people experience heartbreak most of the time but, in some rare cases this even translates to true love

This book is the story of how I went through the pain of that love, I Have included many Shayaris of different poets as we all know Shayari is the language of love. Credits to all those poets

I would like to end this message by saying that people may not succeed on first tries but they do succeed after multiple failures, for failures are the key to success

Foreword

"7 Stages of One-Sided Love" is a poignant and deeply resonant exploration of the complex emotions accompanying loving someone who does not love you back. As a reader who has walked this path, I found solace and understanding in these pages. This book is a journey through the raw, unfiltered stages of unrequited love, beautifully articulated through poetry and prose.

The author begins with infatuation, capturing the excitement and possibility of those initial feelings. The butterflies, the racing heart, and the overwhelming desire to be near the object of your affection are vividly described, bringing back memories of my own early experiences with unreciprocated love.

The second stage, longing, delves into the persistent yearning for the person you love. This part of the book resonated deeply with me as it articulated the sleepless nights and endless daydreams I once experienced. The author's words echo the constant ache of missing someone who may not even know you exist.

As the book progresses to obsession, the intensity of the feelings is palpable. The author skillfully captures the all-consuming thoughts and the desperate hope for even the smallest interaction. This stage blurs the line between admiration and fixation, reflecting a time when my thoughts were entirely dominated by someone who barely noticed me.

Hope, the next stage, is a delicate balance of optimism and despair. The author perfectly encapsulates the fragile belief that your feelings might be reciprocated, along with the fear of inevitable disappointment. This stage is fraught with uncertainty and the poignant dreams of what could be.

Heartbreak is the most painful stage, where the harsh reality of unrequited love sinks in. The author's depiction of shattered dreams and overwhelming sorrow brought tears to my eyes, as it mirrored my own experiences of deep emotional pain and loss. Yet, this stage is also a crucible of growth and transformation.

Death, in the literal sense, follows heartbreak. The author bravely addresses this stage, where the weight of unrequited love becomes too much to bear. This stage is a sobering reminder of the profound impact that unreciprocated feelings can have on a person's mental and emotional well-being. It is a stage that speaks to the ultimate price some pay for their silent love, a stark confrontation with the finality of life and the unbearable pain of a broken heart.

The final stage, growth, is where the true beauty of this book shines. Even after death, the narrative continues, reflecting on the lives of those left behind and the enduring legacy of the one who loved in silence. The author explores how others find strength and wisdom in the wake of loss, using the pain of unrequited love as fuel for creativity and personal development. This stage is a testament to the resilience of the human spirit and the transformative power of love, even when it ends in tragedy.

"7 Stages of One-Sided Love" is not just a book about the pain of unrequited love; it is a celebration of its transformative power. It is a testament to the strength and resilience found within the human spirit. The author's journey through these stages mirrors my own, and I found comfort in knowing that I was not alone in my experiences.

This book offers a voice to those who have loved in silence, providing a sense of understanding and validation.

The author's ability to express the inexpressible through poetry and prose is a gift to anyone who has felt the sting of unrequited love.

As you embark on this journey through the seven stages, may you find the same solace and understanding that I did. Whether you are in the throes of infatuation, the depths of heartbreak, or grappling with the reality of death, know that every stage is a part of the greater tapestry of life. Let this book be a guide, a companion, and a source of comfort as you navigate the complex emotions of one-sided love.

With heartfelt gratitude,
A Fellow Traveler in Love

CHAPTER ONE

ATTRACTION

I came into the world crying, while everyone around me was smiling. But what do you expect from a baby seeing the light of day for the first time? Growing up, I was always pampered being the only child till the time my cousin was born; with him came the oldest child treatment. He was always given priority in everything, whether it be chores, vacations, or even toys. I hated him at the time, but now I understand the reason for that treatment. Growing up, I never thought life was worth living until she came into my life. It was sudden, and I didn't even understand when I had a crush on her. I would say that it was a love-at-first-sight moment—the moment she made eye contact with me—you know, I was visibly red and blushing; it was around September at that time. My class teacher came to the class and announced that she needed tall boys for our school's annual function and me being the boy of ego raised that hand as high as I could, lucky for me she noticed that hand of mine and I was the first to be called upon, I along with 12 others of various classes went to the dance room, There I met her for the first time, her eyes were like an ocean—deep, vast, and endless. Her grace carried a whole century's worth of elegance, and her hair was pure silk., I never thought that I would fall in love at 14 or while studying in class 8 for god's sake but, I guess life had other plans for me, my honest opinion for her cannot be in words it has to be a sher this was my very first and also a start of many more-

> *" "Jab kabhi khuda ne banaya hoga use fursat mein.*
> *Aakho mein samandar aur adao mein puri kainat bharke*
> *Sach kehta hu us khuda ka bhi imann dagmagaya hoga*
> *tujhe iss dharti par bhejte bhejte." "*

Well, she was my world at the time; nights were filled with her dreams, and the days were spent just practicing for the function. The year was coming to an end, and I was falling deeper into the hole of love.

The realisation that I was sharing the stage with her added another layer of excitement to the upcoming school function. As the days dwindled to the grand event, the dance rehearsals became even more special as I now shared the stage, practicing together and exchanging smiles that spoke volumes without uttering a single word.

The synchronicity in the dance moves mirrored the connection that I dreamed about every night. There was an unspoken understanding that transcended the choreography—a silent communication through glances and shared laughter that only I could comprehend; it was the greatest feeling in the world.

The air was charged with a blend of nerves and excitement on the night of the function. As we took our respective positions on stage, the spotlight illuminated. Not just me, but every single human on that stage was nervous.

The dance floor became a canvas where the unspoken emotions painted a story of budding affection.

Amid the performance, as I moved in rhythm with the music, my eyes sought hers at the back of the stage. The shared spotlight felt like a metaphor for the shared experience unfolding between us. The applause from the audience served as an acknowledgement not only of the well-executed dance but also of the hours of practice that went in, but I did not care because all for me was that I was sharing the stage with her.

After the performance, amidst the applause and congratulatory messages, we shared glances. The smiles we exchanged were not just about the success of the dance; they carried the weight of shared accomplishment and the beginning of something special.

The post-function celebration became a backdrop for more shared moments as the night unfolded. The laughter, the camaraderie, and the joy of a successful performance bonded us two in a way that was beyond the reach of words. Little did I know that this shared stage experience was merely the overture to a larger symphony of emotions and shared adventures that awaited me in the chapters yet to unfold.

As the final notes of the school function faded into the night, a chapter of my life began—a chapter on one-sided love. It was during that enchanting evening that our eyes first met, and our hearts began to beat in unison. Love, like a flickering flame, danced in the air, igniting an emotional storm within me. Little did I know that those stolen glances would become the highlight of my nights as I yearned for a love that could never be returned.

Every time our eyes met, it felt like time stood still. In those fleeting moments, I could see the reflection of my longing mirrored in her gaze. But alas, it was not meant to be. While my heart soared to unimaginable heights, hers remained unyielding, unaware of the emotions that consumed my every waking thought. Love has a way of playing cruel tricks on the unsuspecting soul, leaving them vulnerable and exposed.

The days turned into weeks, and the weeks into months. Yet, my love for her remained steadfast, unyielding to the passage of time. I watched from afar as she laughed with her friends, unaware of the turmoil that raged within me. Each night, I would lie awake, replaying our brief encounters over and over again in my mind. The echoes of her laughter haunted me, filling the empty spaces of my heart with a bittersweet ache.

Oh, how I longed for the courage to confess my love to her! But fear held me captive, trapping my words within the depths of my soul. What if she rejected me? What if our friendship became nothing more than a distant memory? These questions tormented me day and night as I battled with the overwhelming desire to pour out my heart to her.

And so, my love for her remained hidden in the shadows, forever confined to the depths of secrecy. Each passing day brought with it a new battle—a battle between my heart's desires and the reality that stared me in the face. But even though our love was unrequited, it did not diminish its intensity. Instead, it grew stronger with each passing moment, intertwining itself with every fibre of my being.

In this chapter on one-sided love, I learnt that love is not always reciprocated. It is not always fair or just. It can leave one vulnerable and exposed, like a wounded bird with broken wings. But despite the pain and heartache that come with unrequited love, there is beauty in its rawness and vulnerability. That was the time I understood how hard falling in love is.

At night, I'd lie awake, scrolling through old photos of the function, reliving every glance she threw my way. I used to write a diary to deal with these, and one of the entries I wrote on those long nights is

"In the darkness of the night, my heart beats with a fervour that cannot be contained. Each thump echoes through my chest, a constant reminder of the love that consumes me. It is a one-sided love—a love that burns within me while remaining unrequited. But still, I hold on, hoping that one day my feelings will be reciprocated.

As the moon casts its gentle glow upon my face, I am overcome with memories of our interactions. Every stolen glance, every accidental touch, they play on repeat in my mind like a broken record. Each memory becomes etched into the deepest recesses of my heart, fuelling the fire of my unrequited affection. It is in these moments, in the silence of the night, that I allow myself to indulge in the sweet agony of my unfulfilled desires.

And oh, how I long to gaze into her eyes once again. Those eyes, so captivating and full of depth, have left an indelible mark on my soul. They hold a power over me that I cannot escape—a magnetic pull that draws me closer despite the pain it inflicts. In the stillness of the night, I search for consolation within those eyes, hoping to find a flicker of recognition, a sign that my love has not been in vain.

But as the night wears on and the darkness deepens, reality begins to seep in. The truth becomes harder to ignore with each passing moment. I am but a mere spectator in her life, an extra in the grand play of her existence. My love remains unacknowledged and unreciprocated, a silent ache that threatens to consume me whole.

So here I remain, hidden beneath the cover of the night, wrestling with the turmoil of my one-sided love. The beating of my heart serves as a constant reminder of what could have been and what should have been. But alas, it is not meant to be.

Yet still, I find comfort in these nights of longing. For in the darkness, amongst the shadows, I can hold onto the hope that one day she will see me, truly see me. Until then, I will continue to bear the weight of this unrequited affection, cherishing each moment we share in my dreams and praying for the day when our paths may intertwine once more."

As the days stretched into weeks and the weeks into months, the weight of unrequited love bore down on me like a heavy cloak, enveloping me in a shroud of longing and uncertainty. Each passing moment seemed to magnify the chasm between us, a divide forged by the unspoken words that lingered between our fleeting glances.

In the quiet solitude of the night, when the world around me faded into darkness and the stars whispered secrets to the moon, I found myself grappling with the relentless tide of emotions that threatened to engulf me. It was in those solitary moments that the ache of unfulfilled desires echoed loudest, reverberating through the chambers of my heart with a haunting intensity.

Yet, amidst the shadows of longing, there existed a glimmer of hope—a fragile thread that bound me to the possibility of a love yet unexplored. It was a beacon of light in the darkness, a whisper of possibility that danced on the edges of my consciousness, teasing me with the tantalising prospect of reciprocated affection.

And so I clung to that hope like a lifeline, allowing it to guide me through the labyrinth of uncertainty that defined our relationship. With each passing day, I found solace in the simple act of dreaming—of envisioning a future where our hearts beat in unison, where our souls intertwined in a symphony of love and devotion.

But as the sands of time continued to slip through the hourglass, reality remained steadfast in its refusal to bend to the whims of my desires. The gulf between us widened with each passing moment, a silent testament to the barriers that stood between us—a testament to the complexities of the human heart and the intricacies of unspoken emotions.

In the depths of my longing, I found myself grappling with the age-old question of fate versus free will—of whether our destinies were predetermined by forces beyond our control or if we held the power to shape our paths. It was a question that lingered on the fringes of my consciousness, a spectre that haunted the recesses of my mind with its unanswerable riddles.

And yet, despite the uncertainty that shrouded our connection, I could not deny the profound impact she had on my life. Her presence was a balm to my wounded soul, a beacon of light in the darkest corners of my despair. With each passing day, she became more than a mere object of affection—she became a symbol of hope, a testament to the enduring power of love in all its myriad forms.

In the tapestry of our shared experiences, I found moments of fleeting joy—moments where our laughter mingled in the crisp night air, where our conversations flowed like rivers of understanding, where the barriers that separated us seemed to fade into insignificance. It was in those moments that I glimpsed the true depth of our connection, a connection that transcended the boundaries of time and space.

But even as I basked in the warmth of her presence, I could not escape the gnawing ache of unfulfilled desires—the haunting spectre of what could have been if only our paths had aligned in a different time, a different place. It was a thought that lingered on the periphery of my consciousness, a reminder of the fragile nature of human connection and the fleetingness of our mortal existence.

And so I resigned myself to the ebb and flow of fate, surrendering to the currents of destiny that carried us ever further apart. For in the tapestry of our shared experiences, I found solace in the knowledge that our love, though unrequited, would forever endure—a timeless testament to the beauty of human connection and the resilience of the human spirit.

As the night wore on and the darkness deepened, I found comfort in the quiet solitude of my longing—a silent symphony of unspoken words and unfulfilled dreams. And though the road ahead remained uncertain, I took comfort in the knowledge that love, in all its myriad forms, would forever illuminate the darkest corners of my heart—a beacon of hope in a world shrouded in shadow.

Every one of my friends knew about her and even some of my seniors; frankly, just two people remembered it first: my best friend at the time, Sayurjo, and my bus senior, Kustav. They were like my brothers; I used to talk to them every day, in school or on WhatsApp or Instagram. They were the only ones who frankly knew every detail of my life.

Sometimes I think about what attraction is or why I got attracted to her, and I think I know the answer after 2 years of that first sight. Attraction is an enigmatic force that captivates the soul and ignites a fire within. It is a magnetic pull that transcends mere physical beauty and delves into the realm of deeper connection. The allure lies not only in her captivating smile and alluring curves but also in the profound essence that emanates from within. It is the way her eyes shimmer with intelligence and curiosity, drawing you into a world of endless possibilities. It is the way her laughter dances through the air, filling your heart with joy and warmth. Attraction to a girl is an inexplicable phenomenon that defies logic and reason, leaving one spellbound and entranced. It is a force that can consume the mind, body, and soul, forever altering the course of one's existence. As it did to me, falling in love changed me. Before this, I never cared about how I looked or felt, but after meeting her, I tried to make myself more presentable,I started combing my hair properly, fixing my tie, checking the mirror twice before leaving for school spoke less, and thought before every action—things I never did before. This made me lose friends, but I did not care; all I cared about was what she would think of me if we ever talked.

> *""Tujhe bin yaad kiye bhula raha hu main*
> *Tujhpe marke zindagi bita raha hu main*
> *Aur tere pyaar ne aisa badla mujhe ki*
> *Teri sari Aadatein apna raha hu main.""*

Love can change people in ways that we never thought were possible because

Love has the power to transform and shape us into entirely different individuals. It is a force that can alter the course of our lives, opening our eyes to new perspectives and possibilities. When love enters our lives, it can change us in profound and unexpected ways. It can break down walls we have built around ourselves, exposing our vulnerabilities and allowing us to grow and evolve.

Before experiencing love, I may have been closed off or hesitant to let others in. I may have carried around emotional baggage, harbouring past hurts and disappointments. However, when love finds its way into our hearts, it has a way of melting away these barriers. Love teaches us to trust again, to believe in the goodness of others, and to be vulnerable. It allows us to let go of our fears and insecurities, enabling us to embrace the joy and beauty that come with truly connecting with another person.

Love also has the power to change our priorities and values. Before falling in love, we may have been focused solely on ourselves and our desires. However, when love enters our lives, it shifts our perspective. Suddenly, the happiness and well-being of our partner become just as important as our own. We become more selfless and willing to make sacrifices for the ones we love. Love teaches us the importance of compromise, understanding, and empathy. It broadens our horizons and encourages us to consider the needs and feelings of others.

Love can also ignite a fire within us, inspiring us to pursue our dreams and become the best versions of ourselves. When someone loves us unconditionally, they see our potential even when we may not see it ourselves. Their belief in us becomes a catalyst for change, encouraging us to step outside of our comfort zones and take risks. Love motivates us to overcome obstacles and challenges, pushing us towards personal growth and self-improvement.

In addition to these internal changes, love can also transform our behaviour towards others. We become more compassionate, patient, and understanding. Love teaches us to be kinder and more forgiving, as we recognise that everyone makes mistakes and deserves a second chance. We become more aware of the impact our words and actions have on those around us, striving to be a source of positivity and support for others.

Love has the power to change us in remarkable ways. It can break down walls, shift our priorities, ignite passion within us, and inspire kindness towards others. When we open ourselves up to love, we allow it to shape us into individuals who are more compassionate, understanding, and driven. Love changes us for the better, making us more aware of the beauty that exists within ourselves and in the world around us.

> *"Mohabbat kalandaro rakhs hai miya.*
> *Yeh laadlo ki bas ki baat*
> *Mohabbat mein aisa uljhe ki sab bhul gaye.*
> *Kya bhule kuch yaad nahi."*

Just like that, we reached the final exams while she was out for the board exams. It felt strange not having her around during such an important time. As the days passed, I almost forgot about her because the workload and stress of the exams consumed my thoughts. The final exams brought an overwhelming schedule with back-to-back papers and extensive study sessions. Each day seemed to blur into the next, and I found myself completely engrossed in the academic challenges that lay ahead. Amidst the chaos of exam preparation, I inadvertently shifted my focus solely to my academic success. With each passing day, her absence became a distant thought as I poured all my energy into my studies. However, just when I thought I had almost forgotten about her, a familiar face reappeared on the day of our last exam. It was her, back from the board exams. Well, she was a board topper, and well, I was not even in the top 10 in class. After that day, I was on vacation for the session break, and just like that, we reached 2023 and class 9.

CHAPTER TWO

AFFECTION

The first day of ninth grade was supposed to be just another day. I walked into the school building, a mix of nerves and excitement clashing within me. Everything was the same: the hallways echoed with familiar voices, the worn-out lockers stood in rows, and the distinct smell of cafeteria food wafted through the air. I thought I knew what to expect—just another start to the school year. But then I saw her.

It felt like someone had hit the rewind button on my life. The world around me blurred, and all I could see was her. That face, that smile—it was as if I had stepped into a memory. Everything came flooding back with such force that I had to steady myself against a locker. She hadn't changed a bit. If anything, she had only grown more radiant over the summer. Her hair, that beautiful cascade of chestnut waves, caught the light as she moved through the crowded hall, laughing with her friends.

It had been almost a year since I last saw her, since I last felt that pull.I thought maybe—just maybe—time and distance would dull the sharp edge of my feelings. But I was wrong. Seeing her now, all those feelings came rushing back, more intense than ever before. My heart raced in my chest, and the poet inside me stirred.

She didn't notice me. Of course, she didn't. Why would she? To her, I was just another face in the crowd. But to me, she was the sun, the moon, the stars. She was everything. I stood frozen in place, watching as she moved with effortless grace, her laughter ringing out like a melody only I could hear.

How could someone have such an effect on me? It was as if she carried a piece of my soul with her, and every time I saw her, that part of me longed to return. But I knew it never would. I knew that this was a one-sided love, a love that would never be returned. And yet, I couldn't help it. I couldn't stop myself from feeling this way, even if it meant torturing myself every time I saw her.

I remember the first time I saw her, back in seventh grade. I was just another kid in a sea of faces for her. But from the moment she walked into my life, I was captivated. She had this way of making everything around her seem brighter as if the world itself revolved around her. And maybe for me, it did.

I would watch her from afar, too shy to ever say anything. Every glance, every smile, every laugh—it was all burned into my memory. I would write about her in my journal, scribbling down poems that no one would ever read. I poured all my feelings into those pages, knowing that they would never amount to anything more than ink on paper. But it was all I had. It was the only way I knew how to cope with the overwhelming emotions that threatened to consume me.

Now, standing in the hallway of our school, those feelings came rushing back with a vengeance. I wanted to look away, to turn and walk in the opposite direction, but I couldn't. My feet were glued to the floor, and my eyes locked on her as she moved through the crowd. It was as if time had stopped, and I was the only one frozen in place, watching as she drifted further and further away from me.

I knew this year would be different. Ninth grade marked the start of something new, something bigger. We were no longer kids in middle school—we were high schoolers now, on the cusp of adulthood. But for me, it felt like nothing had changed. I was still the same awkward, lovesick boy, hopelessly infatuated with a girl who didn't even know I existed.

As I stood there, lost in thought, the bell rang, snapping me back to reality. I hurried to my classroom, hoping to shake off the feelings that had overwhelmed me. But no matter how hard I tried, I couldn't stop thinking about her. She was like a song stuck in my head, playing on a loop, haunting me with every note.

The classroom was a blur. I sat at my desk, staring blankly at the blackboard as the teacher droned on about school policies and upcoming events. I couldn't focus. All I could think about was her—where she was, what she was doing, who she was with. Was she thinking about me, even for a second? No, of course not. She didn't even know I was there.

But that didn't stop the poet inside me from stirring again. Words began to form in my mind, words that I knew I would write down later when I was alone. Words that would capture the way she made me feel, the way she always had.

The days passed, and I settled into the routine of school. Classes, homework, lunch with friends—it was all the same as it had been before. But now, there was an added weight to everything. Every day, I saw her. Sometimes it was just a fleeting glance in the hallway, other times I would spot her across the canteen, laughing with her friends. And every time, it was like a punch to the gut.

I kept my distance, as I always had. What else could I do? She was untouchable, like some kind of distant star. I could admire her from afar, but I could never reach her. And yet, I couldn't stop myself from hoping. I couldn't stop myself from dreaming that maybe, just maybe, she would notice me. That one day, she would look my way and see me for who I was.

But that day never came. Instead, I spent my time writing. Every night, after finishing my homework, I would sit at my desk and let the words flow. I wrote about her smile, her laugh, the way her eyes sparkled in the sunlight. I wrote about the way she made me feel, the way she made my heart ache with longing. And as the days turned into weeks, those words piled up, filling page after page with the story of my one-sided love.

October arrived, and with it came the chill of autumn. The leaves turned shades of red and gold, and the air grew crisp and cool. The change in season brought with it a sense of melancholy that seemed to seep into my bones. I watched as couples held hands in the hallways, laughing and smiling as they walked together. I watched as friends made plans for parties and bonfires, their excitement palpable.

And there I was, alone, always on the outside looking in. It wasn't that I didn't have friends—I did. But no matter how hard I tried to distract myself, I couldn't escape the feeling of emptiness that gnawed at me. I wanted more than anything to be with her, to be the one making her laugh, the one walking beside her, holding her hand. But that was just a fantasy, a dream that would never come true.

As the days grew shorter and the nights longer, I found myself retreating more and more into my writing. The poet inside me had taken over completely, and I poured all my feelings into my journal. I wrote about the changing seasons, about the way the leaves fell from the trees like broken promises. I wrote about the chill in the air, the way it reminded me of the coldness of unrequited love. There were moments, brief and fleeting, when I would catch her looking my way. I would hold my breath, my heart pounding in my chest, hoping that maybe this time, she would see me. But those moments never lasted. She would turn away, her attention elsewhere, and I would be left with nothing but the lingering ache of what could never be.

Weeks passed in a haze of routines, distant glances, and quiet yearning. The weather turned colder, leaves continued to fall, and with each gust of wind, it felt like a piece of me was drifting further away from reality. October, a month that once promised the excitement of festivities and the magic of autumn, now felt like an endless stretch of longing.

The brief interaction with her that day—the returned paper, the fleeting smile—had become my anchor. I clung to that moment, replaying it over and over in my mind, convincing myself that it meant something. But as the days went on, it became clear that nothing had changed. She hadn't spoken to me again, hadn't even looked in my direction. To her, I was just another anonymous face in the crowd.

Still, I couldn't shake the hope that had taken root inside me. I would find myself scanning the hallways between classes, searching for her in the sea of students. Sometimes I would catch a glimpse of her—laughing with her friends, her hair catching the light in that same mesmerizing way. Other times, I would see her sitting at a table in the canteen, surrounded by people, her attention always elsewhere.

But no matter how hard I tried to convince myself that she was out of reach, that my feelings were nothing more than a hopeless crush, I couldn't let go. She was always there, in the back of my mind, a constant presence that shaped every thought, every action.

One day, in mid-October, something unusual happened. I was sitting at my desk in English class, doodling absentmindedly in my notebook while the teacher explained the nuances of Shakespeare's Romeo and Juliet. Normally, I would have been paying close attention—it was, after all, one of my favorite plays—but today, my mind was elsewhere.

I kept thinking about her, about that smile, about the way she had handed me that page from my journal without saying a word. I wondered what would have happened if I had been braver, if I had taken that moment to talk to her instead of retreating into my shell.

Suddenly, the teacher's voice cut through my thoughts.

"We're going to do something a little different today," she said, her eyes scanning the room. "Since we're studying Romeo and Juliet, I want each of you to pair up with a classmate and work on a short scene together. You'll have the next couple of days to prepare, and then you'll perform the scene in front of the class."

A murmur of excitement ran through the room. I felt my stomach sink. I wasn't great at performing in front of people, especially not when it came to something as emotional as Romeo and Juliet. And on top of that, the idea of partnering up with someone sent a wave of anxiety through me.To add insult to injury I could not get those imaginations about her out of my head

As October moved forward, the crisp air took on a sharper chill, reminding me that the coldest days were yet to come. The school was a mix of monotony and fleeting moments where I would catch glimpses of her in the halls or across the courtyard. Nothing more had happened between us since that day in September when she returned my lost page, and I knew better than to expect anything else.

Classes continued as usual, and I did my best to focus on assignments and group projects. But no matter how hard I tried, thoughts of her were always lurking in the background, especially when I found myself lost in the quiet moments between tasks.

I remember sitting in English class one afternoon, feeling particularly disconnected. The teacher had been going on about classic literature, and my mind drifted as I stared at the space between the window and the desk in front of me. Outside, the leaves swirled in chaotic patterns, carried by the autumn wind.

It was then that I caught a glimpse of her through the window. She was walking across the courtyard, her head tilted back in laughter, her arm looped around the shoulders of one of her friends. That familiar ache returned to my chest, the one that had become all too familiar over the past two years. She was always so full of life, so out of reach, like a star I could only admire from afar.

I quickly looked away, feeling the now-constant mixture of longing and hopelessness. It was becoming clear to me that this was how things would be: I'd observe her from a distance, stuck in a loop of wanting and never getting close enough to change anything.

As Puja approached, the school buzzed with the excitement of upcoming parties and plans for the weekend. My friends were discussing which events they would attend, but I wasn't in the mood. The idea of dressing up and pretending to enjoy myself in a crowded room filled with people who wouldn't even notice me felt exhausting. I was tired of standing on the edges of things, always watching but never really participating.

On the Friday before Holidays, I found myself back in the school library during lunch, once again retreating from the noise of the cafeteria. I hadn't been able to shake the thought of her all day, and it weighed on me like a stone tied to my chest.

I opened my journal and began to write again, letting the words spill out onto the page:

> *""Like the moon watching the sun,*
> *I orbit, but we never meet.*
> *Your light warms others, but leaves me cold,*
> *Always at a distance, always incomplete.""*

The pen glided across the paper, but even the act of writing didn't feel like enough anymore. It had been my way of processing, of coping, but now, it just felt like I was going in circles, writing the same story over and over again.

As I closed the journal and leaned back in my chair, I caught sight of her walking past the library door. She didn't come inside, didn't even look in my direction, but that brief second was enough to send my heart racing again. I wondered where she was headed, and what her plans were for the weekend. Was she going to a party? Would she be out with friends? And, once again, would I be alone, thinking about her while she remained oblivious to my existence?

By the time Puja arrived, I had resigned myself to spending the night at home. My friends had tried to convince me to come to a party, but I made some excuses about being too tired or having too much homework. It wasn't entirely a lie—I did have an essay to finish—but the truth was, I just didn't feel like pretending to be someone I wasn't for a night.

I sat in my room, the soft glow of my desk lamp illuminating the pages of my journal as I wrote through the sounds of children trick-or-treating outside. Their laughter and the occasional shout of "trick or treat" filtered through the window, but inside, it was quiet.

> *""I wonder if you're laughing tonight,*
> *I wonder if you know how your smile haunts me,*
> *Or if I'm just a shadow in the crowd,*
> *Another face you'll never see.""*

I paused, staring at the words, wondering how much longer I could go on like this. How long could I keep writing about someone who would never know how I felt?

As October moved forward, the crisp air took on a sharper bite, reminding me that the coldest days were yet to come. The anticipation of winter was hanging in the atmosphere—leaves in shades of amber, crimson, and gold fell in quiet spirals, and everything seemed to slow down, preparing for the inevitable stillness that winter brings.

School became a strange mix of monotony and fleeting moments where I caught glimpses of her in the halls or across the courtyard. It was as if my entire day rotated around those brief sightings. Sometimes I would hear her voice as she walked past, laughing with her friends, her footsteps echoing faintly behind her. I didn't have any classes with her, and while the logical part of me knew that was for the best, my heart still ached every time I saw her from afar, longing for even a word, a glance, anything that could bridge the gulf between us.

Nothing more had happened between us since that day in September when she returned my lost page. As far as I could tell, she had forgotten about it entirely. And why wouldn't she? It had been nothing—a brief moment in time that meant the world to me but likely nothing at all to her. I knew better than to expect anything else. I knew better than to hope for more.

Yet, hope had this strange way of clinging on, even when it had no right to. It whispered to me, quiet but persistent, telling me that maybe, just maybe, she would notice me one day. Maybe something would change. Maybe there would come a moment when the universe shifted, and she would see me standing there in the same hallway, day after day, writing about her, dreaming about her.

I shook those thoughts away as quickly as they came. It was too much to hope for. Too much to ask of someone who didn't even know I existed.

The days blurred together in the way that they often do when you're not really living in the moment but instead constantly waiting for something to happen. Classes became routine—math, science, history—all blending into one another. I spent more time staring out the window than I did listening to the teachers. I'd catch sight of her every now and then, walking across the courtyard or sitting with her friends at lunch, and each time I saw her, my chest tightened with that familiar feeling, the one that I had come to accept as part of me.

I remember one particular afternoon in English class. We were reading some classic novel, but I wasn't paying attention. My eyes were drawn to the window, where the branches of a tree swayed in the wind, the last of its leaves clinging desperately to the brittle limbs. Through the swaying branches, I caught a glimpse of her. She was outside, walking across the courtyard with a group of friends, her laughter ringing out, carried on the breeze. She was always laughing, always smiling, and it made my heart ache in a way that was almost unbearable. There was something so effortless about her happiness, something so distant from my own quiet longing.

I watched her for what felt like hours, though it was likely only seconds before she disappeared from view. I turned back to my desk, the teacher's voice a distant hum in the background, and I picked up my pen, letting the words flow across the page:

> *"Like a breeze you pass through my world,*
> *Leaving me gasping for air.*
> *You shine like the sun,*
> *But I remain in the shadows."*

I scribbled down the lines, feeling the weight of each word as if they were carved into me. It had become my ritual—writing about her, letting the emotions spill onto paper because I had nowhere else to put them. It was the only way I knew how to deal with the endless yearning, the endless silence.

As Puja approached, the school was buzzing with excitement. Talk of parties filled the hallways, and everywhere I turned, people were making plans for the weekend. My friends were no exception, eagerly discussing their costumes and which parties they'd be going to. They tried to convince me to join them, but I wasn't in the mood. The thought of dressing up and pretending to have fun at some crowded party didn't appeal to me. How could I have fun when the only thing on my mind was her? I was tired of pretending. Tired of standing on the edges of things, always watching but never really part of the action.

On the Friday before Puja, I found myself once again in the library during lunch. The cafeteria had become overwhelming—a cacophony of laughter and chatter that I couldn't bear to be around. It was too much. I didn't want to see her laughing with her friends, didn't want to watch from a distance as the world moved on without me. So, I retreated to the quiet of the library, where I could lose myself in the solitude of books and the pages of my journal.

I found a corner by the window, far from the few students scattered throughout the room. I opened my journal and stared at the blank page, but for once, the words wouldn't come. The usual flood of emotions felt stifled, blocked by a heaviness that settled deep in my chest. I sighed, leaning back in my chair and rubbing my eyes. Outside, the wind howled, rattling the windows, and I could see the leaves swirling in chaotic patterns across the school grounds.

I thought about her—where she was, what she was doing, what her plans were for the weekend. Was she going to a party? Would she be laughing and dancing with friends while I sat here, alone in the library, lost in my own head?

The thought made my chest ache. It was always like this—watching from the sidelines, imagining what her life must be like, wondering if she was happy, wondering if she ever thought about me. But of course, she didn't. Why would she? To her, I was just another face in the crowd. Just another person walking through the same hallways. Nothing more.

I picked up my pen and began to write, the words coming slowly at first, then faster as the emotions began to pour out:

""You live in a world I can only observe,
A world of laughter and light.
I live in the shadows,
Where silence is my only friend.""

Puja came and went, a blur of costumes and laughter that I observed from a distance. I didn't go to any parties, didn't dress up, didn't participate in any of the festivities. Instead, I spent the night at home, sitting at my desk with my journal open, the sounds of trick-or-treaters echoing faintly from outside. Their laughter and shouts of "trick or treat" filtered through the window, but inside, it was quiet. Too quiet.

I stared at the blank page for what felt like hours, trying to find the words to express how I felt. But nothing seemed right. Nothing seemed to capture the depth of the emptiness inside me. I thought about her, about where she might be, what she might be doing. I imagined her at a party, dressed in some clever costume, surrounded by friends, her laughter filling the room. I imagined her happiness, so far removed from my own loneliness.

Finally, I picked up my pen and began to write, the words heavy and slow:

""Tonight, you are a star in someone else's sky,
Laughing, shining, living.
And I am nothing but a distant observer,
Wishing on a star that will never fall.""

The words felt raw, like they had been torn from some deep part of me that I didn't even know existed. I closed the journal, pushing it away, and leaned back in my chair, staring up at the ceiling. The loneliness was suffocating, wrapping around me like a thick fog that I couldn't escape. I wanted to scream, to shout, to do something—anything—that would make this feeling go away. But I knew it wouldn't. This was my reality. This was how it would always be.

November arrived with a cold, biting wind that seemed to cut through everything. The days grew shorter, the sky darker, and the weight of winter settled over the school like a blanket of silence. The excitement of Puja had faded, replaced by the quiet anticipation of the holidays. But for me, nothing had changed. I was still stuck in the same cycle of longing and silence, watching her from afar, writing about her in my journal, living in a world where she would never know how I felt.

I saw her often in the halls, laughing with friends, her smile lighting up the dreary days. Sometimes I would catch a glimpse of her across the canteen and for a brief moment, our eyes would meet. But it was always the same—she would glance my way, then look past me, as if I were invisible, as if I didn't exist.

I had grown used to it by now. The feeling of being unnoticed, unseen. It was a constant companion, like a shadow that followed me wherever I went.

But even though I had grown used to it, it didn't make it any easier. The ache in my chest was still there, always there, a reminder of the distance between us, a distance that I could never cross.

And so, I did what I always did. I wrote.

The cold, the darkness, the distance—it all became too much, and one day in early November, I found myself retreating to the library again. The library had become my sanctuary, a place where I could hide from the world, from the noise, from the overwhelming weight of my own feelings.

I sat at my usual spot by the window, my journal open in front of me, but the words wouldn't come. I was tired. I'm tired of writing the same things over and over again, tired of the endless cycle of hope and disappointment.

I closed the journal and leaned back in my chair, staring out at the grey sky. The wind howled outside, the trees swaying in the bitter cold. Inside, it was quiet. Too quiet.

And then, in the silence, I saw her.

She was walking past the library window, her head bent against the wind, her coat pulled tight around her. For a moment, I thought she might look up, that our eyes might meet through the glass. But she didn't. She walked on, disappearing from view, leaving me with nothing but the memory of her passing.

I sighed, the ache in my chest heavier than ever.

Days passed, and I continued to watch from the sidelines, writing, dreaming, hoping. But deep down, I knew that nothing would change. I would always be the observer, the silent admirer, the one who saw her but was never seen. Well, this was **love**

LOVE

It was November, and the world around me began to change. The air grew colder, and the days shorter, but the warmth in my heart remained, focused entirely on her. She was the first thought in the morning, the last before I closed my eyes at night. My feelings had grown stronger each month, yet they were confined within the walls of my heart—a love that she would never know.

November was when I noticed the little things even more—the way her hair caught the light and her laughter seemed to lift the spirits of everyone around her. We would exchange polite greetings, our conversations light and friendly, but there was a distance that I couldn't bridge. I found myself lingering on her words long after our encounters, dissecting every smile, every glance, searching for signs that might suggest she felt the same. But all I found was a mirror reflecting my hopes.

The days were growing shorter, and with each sunset, I felt the weight of unspoken emotions pressing down on me. There was something about the way the light faded earlier and earlier that seemed to mirror the sinking feeling in my chest. My friends noticed that I was quieter, more withdrawn, but I couldn't bring myself to explain why. How could I tell them that my thoughts were consumed by someone who barely knew I existed beyond casual acquaintance?

One day, as I walked through the school hallways, I saw her laughing with a group of friends. Her joy was infectious, and even from a distance, it was impossible not to smile at the sound. I wished, more than anything, that I could be part of that laughter, part of her world. But instead, I kept my distance, a silent observer in the life of the girl who had unknowingly captured my heart.

In the days leading up to the school's Annual Day function, the atmosphere at school was buzzing with excitement. Everyone was involved in some activity—preparing for performances, setting up decorations, or coordinating various events. The Annual Day was a big deal, and it was the talk of the school for weeks. My English teacher, had called me to discuss something important.

"Can you come to the staff room during lunch?" she had asked earlier that day. Her tone was serious, yet there was a hint of something I couldn't quite place.

I had no idea what it could be about, but I nodded, agreeing to meet her. She was one of the most respected teachers in school, known for her sharp mind and keen sense of judgment. If she wanted to talk to me, it had to be something significant.

As the lunch bell rang, I made my way to the staff room, weaving through the throngs of students who were either headed to the cafeteria or outside to enjoy their break. My mind raced with possibilities—had I done something wrong? Was she going to assign me some extra work? The uncertainty gnawed at me.

When I arrived at the staff room, she was waiting by the door. She smiled warmly and gestured for me to come in.

The room was filled with the usual chatter of teachers, but she led me to a quiet corner away from the others.

"Thank you for coming," she began. "I've been thinking about the Annual Day function, and I believe you'd be perfect for a particular role."

I blinked, taken aback. "A role?"

"Yes, we need someone to do the voice-over for a character. You have a good voice, and I think you'd do a fantastic job," she explained. "It's an important part of the event, and I believe you're up to the task."

The idea of doing a voice-over intrigued me. It was an opportunity to be involved in the event without being in the spotlight, which suited me perfectly. I wasn't the type to seek attention, preferring to stay in the background. But what sealed the deal was the thought that she, the girl who had captured my heart, would be participating in the function.

She was the best dancer in school, and I knew she would be part of one of the main performances. The idea of being involved in something she was part of, even in a small way, filled me with a sense of anticipation. So, without hesitation, I agreed.

The next couple of days were spent in rehearsals. I would meet with my on-screen actor, practicing my lines and ensuring the timing was perfect. It was tiring work, but I didn't mind. Every minute spent in those rehearsals brought me closer to her, even if only by proximity. I would catch glimpses of her practising her dance routine, her movements graceful and fluid, as if she were made for the stage. She was always surrounded by her friends and admirers, her laughter echoing through the auditorium.

Each day, I would arrive at the rehearsal early, hoping to catch a moment with her, even if it was just a fleeting exchange of pleasantries. And each day, I would leave with my heart a little heavier, weighed down by the realization that my feelings were growing stronger, yet still locked away, unspoken.

As the days passed, the rehearsals became more intense. The Annual Day was just around the corner, and everyone was working hard to make sure everything was perfect. My role, though small, required precision. I had to coordinate with the backstage crew, ensure that my voice-over matched the cues, and work closely with the event organizers.

Through all of this, she was never far from my thoughts. Watching her rehearse was both a joy and a torment. Her passion for dance was evident in every movement, and it was clear that she loved what she was doing. I admired her dedication, and her commitment to perfecting every step. It made me fall for her even more if that was even possible.

One evening, as the rehearsal was winding down, I found myself alone in the auditorium. Everyone else had left, but I lingered, not ready to go home just yet. The auditorium was dimly lit, the stage still bathed in the soft glow of the overhead lights. I walked down the aisle, my footsteps echoing in the space, and stopped at the front row.

I imagined her up on that stage, performing for an audience. I imagined the applause that would follow, the cheers of admiration. And then I imagined myself in the audience, just another face in the crowd, watching her from afar, as I always did.

It was a bittersweet thought, knowing that I would never be more than a spectator in her life. But at the same time, I couldn't help but feel grateful for the moments I had, for the chance to be close to her, even if only in this small way.

As the night of the Annual Day approached, my excitement grew. I knew it would be a night to remember, not just for the performances, but for the memories it would create. I spent the final days leading up to the event perfecting my lines, practising with the other performers, and trying to keep my nerves in check.

Finally, the night arrived. The school was abuzz with energy, students and teachers alike preparing for the big event. The auditorium was packed with parents, students, and faculty, all eager to see the performances.

Backstage, the atmosphere was electric. Performers were putting the final touches on their costumes, running through their routines one last time. I was in my little corner, going over my lines, making sure everything was in order. My heart was racing, a mix of excitement and nerves. But beneath it all, there was the same familiar longing, the same unspoken feelings that had been building for months.

As the event began, I took my place, ready to deliver my lines. The show unfolded beautifully, each performance a testament to the hard work and dedication of the students. When it was her turn to take the stage, I held my breath.

She stepped onto the stage, her movements fluid and graceful, commanding the attention of everyone in the room. The audience was captivated, as was I. She danced with a passion that was both mesmerizing and heartbreaking, a reminder of everything I admired about her, and everything I could never have.

When the night finally came to an end, there was a sense of accomplishment in the air. The event had been a success, and everyone was celebrating. But for me, there was a lingering sadness, a realization that the night I had looked forward to for so long was now over. And with it, another chapter in my story of unspoken love.

The days after the Annual Day were quieter, as if the school was catching its breath after the whirlwind of events. I saw her less often now that the rehearsals were over, and that only made the emptiness in my heart more pronounced. I missed the brief moments we shared, even if they were just in passing. The absence of those moments left a void that nothing else seemed to fill.

December arrived, and with it, the festive spirit of the holidays. The school was decorated with lights and ornaments, and there was a sense of joy in the air. But for me, the holidays were a reminder of everything I didn't have. I watched as she and her friends exchanged gifts, as they made plans for the break. I wished I could be part of those moments, but I remained on the sidelines, watching from a distance.

One day, I walked by the school courtyard and saw her sitting with a group of friends, their laughter ringing out in the crisp winter air. She looked so happy, so carefree, and I couldn't help but smile at the sight. But as I watched, a pang of longing shot through me. I wished I could be the one to make her laugh like that, to share those moments with her.

But I knew that wasn't my place. I was just a background character in her story, a passerby in the grand scheme of her life. And as much as I wanted to be more, I had to accept that this was my role—silent, unseen, but always there.

The closer it got to Christmas, the more I found myself lost in thoughts of her. I imagined what it would be like to spend the holidays together, to exchange gifts, to share in the joy of the season. But those were just fantasies, the kind that only deepened the ache in my heart.

Christmas came and went, a blur of family gatherings and celebrations. I tried to enjoy the festivities, to focus on the people around me, but my thoughts always drifted back to her. I wondered how she was spending her time, if she was with her family if she was happy. I wondered if she ever thought of me at all, even for a moment.

As the year drew to a close, I found myself reflecting on the past twelve months. It had been a year of growth, of change, but also a year of unfulfilled longing. I had hoped, at the start of the year, that I might find the courage to tell her how I felt. But as the days turned into weeks, and the weeks into months, that courage never came. Instead, my feelings remained locked away, growing stronger but never finding an outlet.

And then it was New Year's Eve. The world was alive with anticipation, and everyone around me was excited for the fresh start that a new year promised. But I felt only the weight of the past, of a year spent in silent adoration of someone who would never know the depth of my feelings. As midnight approached, I found myself standing apart from the celebration, lost in thoughts of her.

The countdown began, and as the final seconds of 2023 slipped away, I closed my eyes and made a wish. I wished for the strength to let go, to move on, to find peace in the knowledge that some loves are never meant to be. But when the clock struck twelve, and the fireworks lit up the sky, I knew that nothing had changed. My feelings for her were as strong as ever, and I would carry them into the new year, just as I had carried them through the months before.

2024 dawned with the promise of new beginnings, but for me, it was just another chapter in the same story—a story of one-sided love, of longing without end. I knew that I would continue to love her, quietly, from afar because that was all I could do. This love was a part of me now, woven into the fabric of who I was, and though it might never be returned, it was still something beautiful, something worth holding on to.

And so, as the new year began, I found myself unable to let go, despite the passage of time. My feelings for her continued to grow, stronger and more consuming with each passing day. The change of the year didn't mark an end or a resolution; instead, it deepened the connection I felt, even if it was one-sided.

Every moment with her, no matter how fleeting, seemed to leave an indelible mark on my heart. I was drawn to her in ways I couldn't fully understand, and the more I tried to distance myself, the more I found myself captivated by her presence. The seasons would change, and life would go on, but my feelings remained, undiminished and ever-growing, a testament to the power of a love that had taken root deep within me.

Though she might never know, my heart belonged to her, and that truth only became more undeniable as time moved forward. Each day, I woke up with the thought of her, and each night, I went to sleep with her image in my mind. It was as if she had become a part of my very existence, her presence etched into every corner of my soul.

I tried to distract myself, to find solace in other aspects of my life. I threw myself into my studies, into hobbies, into anything that might take my mind off her. But nothing worked. No matter how hard I tried, she was always there, lingering in the back of my mind, a constant reminder of the love I couldn't escape.

As the new year unfolded, I found myself caught in a cycle of hope and despair. There were days when I convinced myself that maybe, just maybe, she might feel the same way. I would replay our interactions in my mind, searching for any hint, any sign that she might see me as more than just a friend. But those moments of hope were fleeting, quickly replaced by the harsh reality that she was out of reach.

I would see her with her friends, laughing, talking, and living her life, and I would feel a pang of jealousy. Not because she was happy, but because I wasn't part of that happiness. I wanted to be the one to make her smile, to share in her joy, but instead, I was left on the outside, watching from a distance.

There were times when I considered telling her how I felt, of laying my heart bare and risking everything. But the fear of rejection, of losing even the small connection we had, held me back. I couldn't bear the thought of her looking at me with pity, of her awkwardly trying to let me down easily. The risk was too great, and so I remained silent, letting my feelings fester in the dark corners of my heart.

As the months went by, the weight of my unspoken love began to take its toll. It was exhausting, carrying this secret, pretending that everything was fine when inside, I was slowly unravelling. I found myself withdrawing from my friends, from my family, from everything that used to bring me joy. I was consumed by the thought of her, and it was suffocating.

But even in the darkest moments, I couldn't let go. There was something about her, something that kept me tethered to this love, no matter how much it hurt. She was a beacon of light in my life, a source of hope in a world that often felt overwhelming. And so, I clung to that hope, even if it was just a fantasy, because it was better than the alternative.

Spring arrived, bringing with it a sense of renewal, of fresh beginnings. The world around me seemed to come alive, with flowers blooming and the air filled with the scent of new growth. But for me, there was no such renewal. My feelings for her remained as strong as ever, a constant reminder that some things never change.

I watched as she embraced the new season, her energy infectious as she threw herself into new activities and new projects. She was always moving forward, always looking ahead, while I was stuck in the past, trapped by my own emotions. It was a painful realization, knowing that while she was thriving, I was barely holding on.

There were moments when I thought I might finally be able to move on, when I convinced myself that I could let go of this love that had consumed me for so long. But those moments were fleeting, and the truth always came crashing back. I couldn't move on because she had become a part of me, and no matter how much I tried, I couldn't erase her from my heart.

And so, I continued to love her, silently, from a distance, as the world around me moved forward. I knew that this love was a burden, a weight that I would carry for as long as it took, but I also knew that it was worth it. Because even though she might never know, even though this love might never be returned, it was still something beautiful, something pure, something that made me feel alive.

As summer approached, the days grew longer, and the sun shone brighter, casting a warm glow over everything. But for me, the warmth of the season only served to highlight the emptiness inside. While others basked in the joy of summer, I was left with the same longing, the same unanswered questions that had plagued me for months.

She seemed to thrive in the spring, her energy boundless as she embraced the freedom of the season. I would see her with her friends, laughing, exploring, and living her life to the fullest, and I couldn't help but feel a pang of envy. She was everything I wanted to be—happy, carefree, unburdened by the weight of unspoken love.

As the school year came to an end, I found myself dreading the session break. While others looked forward to the time off, to vacations and relaxation, I knew that the break would only mean more time alone with my thoughts, and more time to dwell on the feelings I couldn't escape.

The final days of school were bittersweet. There was a sense of finality in the air as if everyone was saying goodbye to a chapter of their lives. But for me, there was no closure, no sense of resolution. My feelings for her were still as strong as ever, and I knew that they would follow me into the summer, just as they had followed me through the rest of the year.

On the last day of school, I watched as she hugged her friends, as they made plans to stay in touch over the summer. I wished I could be part of those plans, but I knew that wasn't my place. I was just a background character in her story, a silent observer in the life of the girl who had unknowingly captured my heart.

As I walked away from the school that day, I couldn't help but feel a sense of loss. It wasn't just the end of the school year, but the end of another chapter in my story of unrequited love. And yet, despite the pain, I knew that I would continue to carry these feelings with me because they had become a part of who I was.

The PTMs were here and I got good grades, just like that came the hopes of people, I was in class 10 .A boards student, butt I was just concerned about her and well there was one emotion that kept me going, It wa.s **hope**

CHAPTER FOUR

HOPE

The summer was ablaze, the heat soaking into every pore of life, but my mind was elsewhere, far removed from the routine that had come to define the start of each school year. I moved through the usual motions—meetings, hallway greetings, endless chatter about the future and what it would hold for everyone except me. My days felt like a series of monotonous scenes, each blending into the next with a sense of futility. I had no real plans for the future, at least not ones that felt solid. I drifted through my life, weighed down by an unspoken melancholy.

And then, there she was.

I had seen her countless times before, but today it was different. Today, something had shifted inside me. It was more than just a passing glance, more than that familiar knot in my chest that tightened every time I saw her. Today, there was a pull, an inexplicable urge to do something—to step out from the shadows and say the things I'd never had the courage to say.

She wasn't looking at me, of course. She was caught up in her world, surrounded by her friends, her laughter ringing out clear and carefree. And yet, I couldn't take my eyes off her. My heart pounded in my chest, louder and louder, as if it knew this was a moment I couldn't afford to let slip by. I had been silent for too long.

I watched her, knowing that she didn't really know I existed. Not in any real way, at least. To her, I was just another face in the crowd, a background character in her vibrant, brilliant life. It was a hard thing to admit to myself—that I had spent so much time thinking about her, dreaming about what it might be like to know her, while she probably hadn't thought about me once.

And yet, here I was, standing at the edge of something. I didn't know what, exactly—maybe it was foolish to even think about approaching her. What could I possibly say? What would she think if I just walked up and tried to talk to her? She'd probably be polite but uninterested. That was the most likely outcome. And yet...

Something inside me refused to let go of the idea. The urge gnawed at me, a constant whisper in the back of my mind telling me that if I didn't do something now, I'd regret it forever. It was irrational; I knew that. I wasn't the kind of person who could change my entire life with one conversation. But I couldn't shake the feeling that today something could be different.

My mind wandered back to all the other moments when I had almost said something but didn't. There were so many of them—fleeting, insignificant interactions that had burned themselves into my memory because I had let them slip by without doing anything.

There was that one time in class when she had asked me a question about a project we were working on. It had been such a simple exchange—just a few words, really. But I had been so nervous, so completely tongue-tied, that I barely managed to get out a coherent response. I spent the rest of the day replaying the moment in my head, wondering what might have happened if I had been braver, if I had used that opportunity to strike up a conversation.

And then there was the time at the café. We had both been standing in line, waiting for our orders, and for a split second, our eyes had met. She smiled—just a small, polite smile, but it had been enough to make my heart race. I wanted to say something then, too, but the words got stuck in my throat. She had turned back to her phone, and the moment was gone.

These memories, small as they were, had stayed with me. They were like stones in my pocket, weighing me down and reminding me of all the times I had let fear keep me silent.

Just as I gathered the last of my courage and took a step forward, I felt a sudden pull from behind. A voice, familiar and filled with exasperation, cut through the noise of my thoughts.

"Don't be an idiot," Sayurjo said, pulling me back. "You can't just walk up to her like that. She doesn't even know who you are."

Sayurjo was the only one who knew about my feelings. He had known for a while, ever since I had accidentally let it slip during a late-night conversation. At first, he had found it amusing, teasing me about my hopeless crush. But over time, his teasing had become more serious, more concerned.

I pulled my arm free from his grasp, annoyed but also painfully aware that he was right. I didn't want to hear it, though. Not now. Not when I was so close to doing something, finally taking a step forward.

"What's the point?" Sayurjo continued. "She's not going to care. You're just setting yourself up for disappointment."

I didn't respond. I couldn't. Because as much as I hated to admit it, I knew he was right. She probably wouldn't care. I was just another person in the crowd to her. But that didn't stop the feeling inside me—the desperate need to do something, anything, to make her see me.

For a moment, I stood there, frozen in place. Sayurjo was still watching me, waiting for me to come to my senses and give up this foolish idea. I could feel the weight of his expectations pressing down on me, telling me to let it go and to stay where I was, safe and unnoticed.

The silence that followed was thick with tension. I stood there, feeling every ounce of uncertainty weighing me down. The very moment I had been building up to seemed to stretch on indefinitely. I could feel Sayurjo's eyes on me, his presence a tangible reminder of the rational voice in the back of my mind.

"Maybe you're right," I said finally, my voice barely more than a whisper. "Maybe I should just—"

Before I could finish, Sayurjo gave me a relieved nod. "Thank you," he said, a hint of a smile playing at the corners of his mouth. "I just don't want to see you get hurt."

His words echoed in my head as I turned away from where she stood. I felt a strange mixture of relief and disappointment. Relief because I had avoided the immediate anxiety of a potentially awkward encounter, and disappointment because I was once again backing away from what I truly wanted.

As I walked back, my steps felt lighter, almost as if a burden had been lifted. Yet beneath the surface of this newfound ease was a twinge of regret. I could have taken a chance, made a move, and maybe things could have been different. But fear had won this round, and I was left with the quiet knowledge that the opportunity had slipped through my fingers.

I walked aimlessly through the school grounds, my thoughts swirling around the encounter that almost was. The vibrant scene of students chatting and laughing felt distant and hollow. The joy and energy of the school year seemed to mock me as I replayed the moments in my head.

I passed by familiar landmarks—the old canteen where I used to sit during lunch, the library steps where I often lost myself in books. These were places of comfort, yet today they felt like reminders of my hesitation.

Sayurjo's words replayed in my mind: "She doesn't even know about you." The simple truth of his statement was hard to ignore. I had been living in a fantasy, imagining scenarios where I was more than just a bystander. But the reality was different. I was a stranger to her, an invisible figure in the background of her life.

Later that evening, as I sat alone in my room, the weight of the day pressed heavily on my shoulders. The feeling of missed opportunity was almost physical—a dull ache that lingered. I considered what had happened. I had given in to my fears and Sayurjo's well-meaning advice, but at what cost?

I reached for my journal, a habit I had developed over the years to process my thoughts. Writing had always helped me sort through my emotions, and tonight was no different. As I wrote, I reflected on the moments when I had almost made a move but didn't. Each time, I rationalized my decision and told myself it wasn't the right time or that I wasn't ready.

But was I ever going to be ready? Or was I simply afraid of taking a chance?

The entry was raw and honest, filled with frustration and self-doubt. It ended with a question that lingered in my mind: Was this the life I wanted, a life of missed opportunities and regrets?

As the days passed, the weight of my decision began to set in. Each time I saw her around school, I felt a pang of regret. The feeling was almost unbearable at times, a constant reminder of what could have been.

I began to think about how I could approach this differently. Perhaps it was time to change my strategy. Instead of focusing on the fear of rejection, I needed to focus on what I truly wanted. I started planning small, achievable steps. Maybe it wasn't about making a grand declaration or having an earth-shattering conversation. Maybe it was about starting small—like finding opportunities to interact in casual, non-threatening ways.

I thought about ways to be more present, to engage in conversations where I could slowly build up to something more. I decided to start participating more actively in school events, clubs, and activities that might put me in her path. If I could get to know her naturally, maybe it would be easier to bridge the gap.

In the following weeks, I made a conscious effort to become more involved. I joined a few clubs and participated in school events. Each interaction, each small step, was a way to build confidence and create opportunities for organic conversations. It was a slow process

, and often, I felt like I was just going through the motions.

There were moments of frustration—times when I felt like my efforts were going unnoticed or when I questioned whether this was all worth it. But there were also moments of success—small victories that gave me hope. I started to feel more comfortable in my skin and more confident in my interactions.

As the summer days began to give way to the early hints of fall, I found myself entrenched in the rhythm of a new routine. The warmth of June had not yet fully receded, leaving behind long, languid days that seemed to stretch endlessly. Yet, my thoughts were consumed by a mix of lingering regret and newfound determination.

I had taken Sayurjo's advice to heart, but the sting of missed opportunity lingered. Despite his good intentions, the notion of letting go of what could have been left me grappling with an underlying restlessness. So, I resolved to approach the situation differently, not as a passive observer but as someone willing to engage actively with the world around me.

I began making a deliberate effort to be more visible, to engage with the activities and people that would place me in her orbit. Joining various clubs and participating in school events felt like stepping into a new world, one where I could slowly carve out a space for myself.

Gradually, these small interactions began to build a foundation of familiarity. Each encounter, no matter how brief, added to a growing sense of comfort. I started to notice subtle changes: she would smile when she saw me, or we would exchange a few words in passing. These moments, though minor, were significant to me.

I continued to be active in school activities, attending meetings and participating in events. My increased presence seemed to have an effect—she began to recognize me more, and I felt more at ease around her. It was as if the wall of invisibility was gradually coming down, revealing glimpses of a potential connection.

Despite these small victories, there were moments of doubt. I sometimes wondered if my efforts were enough or if I was just another background figure in her life. The frustration of not knowing where I stood often threatened to overshadow the progress I was making. I questioned whether my efforts were worth it or if I was merely prolonging a cycle of hope and disappointment.

There were days when the weight of these questions felt overwhelming. I would retreat to my journal, pouring out my thoughts and feelings. Writing became a way to process my emotions and to remind myself why I had embarked on this journey in the first place. It was about more than just making a grand gesture—it was about becoming more comfortable in my skin and learning to navigate the complexities of human connection.

By mid-June, I began to reflect on how far I had come. The interactions with her, though not yet profound, had become a regular part of my school life. I felt more confident and less anxious about our conversations. The initial fear of rejection had lessened, replaced by a cautious optimism.

I found myself in a quiet moment, sitting on the steps of the school's old auditorium. The sun was setting, casting a warm glow over the campus. It was one of those rare moments of solitude where I could reflect on my journey. I realized that the pursuit of a deeper connection with her had transformed into a journey of distant love.

I had learned to engage more openly with those around me and had developed a greater sense of confidence. The process had been challenging but also rewarding. I understood that the journey wasn't just about reaching a specific destination but about growing through the experiences along the way.

As June came to a close, I approached the final days of the month with a renewed sense of purpose. I had accepted that the future was uncertain, and that was okay. The journey taught me valuable lessons about patience, self-worth, and the importance of taking chances.

As the month wound up, the pressure of studies was catching up, adding to the uncertainties I faced. The path ahead remained uncertain, but I was slowly descending into **madness**

CHAPTER FIVE

MADNESS

July had arrived like a thief, stealing away the brightness that I used to cling to. This year, the heat didn't feel oppressive, nor did it carry the promise of lazy days by the sea or warm nights under the stars. Instead, it felt hollow, like a worn-out version of something that once had meaning but now didn't. The sun was still there, high in the sky, but its light seemed dimmed as if even it had grown weary of illuminating my life. I could feel it—this emptiness that had settled deep within me, like a pit in my chest that only grew with every passing day.

She was close by, as always, moving with that effortless grace I had come to know so well. But she was also so far away, emotionally distant as if I existed in a completely different world. We shared the same space, and breathed the same air, but the connection I longed for, the bond that would tie me to her, never materialized. And that was the worst part—not that she ignored me, but that I was always there, in the background, unnoticed and unseen, while she continued to shine in her brilliant light.

I would watch her, helpless, as she moved through life. Every laugh she shared with others, every glance she threw in someone else's direction, felt like a dagger lodged deeper into my heart. She radiated joy and energy around others, her laughter a melody that drew people to her effortlessly. But when it came to me, there was nothing. No laughter, no light, just an impenetrable wall I couldn't seem to break through. It was like I had been cast in the role of a mere observer in the story of her life, destined to watch from afar while everyone else took part.

And the worst part was how inescapable she had become. She was everywhere. Even when she wasn't physically there, her presence loomed large in my mind. I couldn't stop thinking about her, couldn't escape the constant reminders of her that seemed to haunt me in every quiet moment. The way her hair shimmered under the sun, how she would close her eyes briefly when she smiled as if savouring the joy of the moment—those details had become etched into my soul. I knew them better than I knew my reflection, and that terrified me.

The distance between us was palpable, like a glass wall that kept me on the outside looking in. I wanted to reach out, to break through, to be part of her world, but no matter how much I tried, I couldn't. She lived in a place that I could never touch, an existence full of light and warmth, while I was stuck in the shadows, fading further with each passing day. She didn't need me. She didn't even know that I existed in the way I needed her to. To her, I was no one, a stranger she passed by without a second thought.

The days stretched on, each one a repeat of the last, an endless cycle of longing and despair. I would wake up with the same hollow feeling in my chest, knowing that nothing would change. I would see her from across the room, hear her voice as she talked to her friends, and feel that familiar ache take hold of me. But she never looked my way. Never noticed the storm of emotions I was drowning in. She didn't need to. She was happy, or at least she seemed that way, and I wasn't part of that happiness.

As July wore on, the long summer evenings that I once loved became unbearable. I used to enjoy how the sun lingered on the horizon, painting the sky in soft hues of gold and pink, the warmth of the day slowly giving way to the cool of the night. But now, those hours felt like a slow, torturous descent into darkness. I would sit alone, watching the world turn to dusk, and all I could think about was how distant she felt. Even when she was just a few feet away, laughing with her friends, she might as well have been a million miles away from me.

The rain started to come more frequently as the days bled into August, the downpours a welcome distraction from the heaviness that weighed on me. But even the rain, with its soothing rhythm and soft, cleansing touch, couldn't wash away the feelings that consumed me. I would sit by the window, watching the droplets slide down the glass, and wonder if she ever thought of me. If, in the quiet moments between her laughter and her conversations, she ever remembered that I existed. But deep down, I knew the answer. I was a passing thought at best, a face in the crowd that held no significance.

August rolled in with a slow, inevitable march, and with it came the realization that nothing was going to change. I had hoped, foolishly, that somehow the distance between us would close, that maybe, just maybe, she would notice me, see me the way I saw her. But as the days went on, it became painfully clear that wasn't going to happen. The gap between us wasn't closing; it was growing wider with every moment of silence, every missed opportunity for connection.

She was always there, living her life as if I didn't exist. And, I was left to watch, to feel the weight of her absence even when she was right in front of me. It was a special kind of torture, being so close to someone and yet feeling like you were a million miles apart. I could see her, hear her, but I couldn't reach her. And that distance—both physical and emotional—was becoming unbearable.

By the time late August arrived, the air had shifted. The once-blistering heat had been replaced by cool breezes, the kind that signalled the slow approach of autumn. It was a relief, in a way, the change in the weather. But it also mirrored the shift I felt inside. The warmth was fading, replaced by something colder, heavier, like a weight I couldn't shake. I would catch glimpses of her—laughing with her friends, smiling in that effortless way that lit up the room—and each time, it felt like a punch to the gut. She was happy, vibrant, and full of life, and I was nothing but a shadow, fading in the background.

The rain came more frequently now as if the sky itself understood the sadness that had settled in my chest. The long, bright days of summer were turning into something else, something greyer, colder, and I couldn't help but feel like it was a reflection of my own heart. She was still there, as beautiful and radiant as ever, but it was as if we were living in separate worlds. She was light, and I was darkness, always following but never quite able to catch up.

I tried to tell myself that this would pass and that eventually, I would stop feeling this way. But with each passing day, the ache in my chest only grew stronger. Every time she passed by without so much as a glance, it felt like another piece of me was being chipped away. It was suffocating, this feeling of longing, of wanting something so badly but knowing you could never have it. I was drowning, and there was no one to pull me out.

There were days when I would sit alone for hours, staring out the window or at the walls, feeling the weight of her absence even though she was still there, just out of reach. The silence between us was deafening, a constant reminder of how insignificant I was in her world. She would smile at others, laugh with them, and share little moments of joy and connection, while for me, there was nothing. Not a word, not a glance. I was invisible.

September crept in quietly, the warmth of summer fading into the crisp, cool bite of autumn. The world around me was changing, moving on, but I was stuck, frozen in place, unable to let go of the feelings that consumed me. The distance between us had become an insurmountable chasm, one that I could never hope to cross. I had hoped, foolishly, that maybe, somehow, things would change. That she would see me, really see me, and that everything would be different.

But now, I knew the truth. She would never see me. Not in the way I saw her. She was a ghost in my life, always present but untouchable, and I was a stranger in hers, someone she would never notice. The realization crushed me. All the hope, all the longing, all the waiting—it had all been for nothing. She didn't care. She never would.

The rain started to fall again, harder this time, as if the sky itself was weeping for me. I sat there, watching her from across the street as she laughed with her friends, her face glowing with a happiness I could never give her. And in that moment, I knew—I would never be part of her world. She would never be mine. I was invisible, and I always would be.

The pain of that realization was overwhelming, but there was nothing I could do. I couldn't make her see me, couldn't force her to care. So I sat there, alone, in the rain, watching her life unfold from a distance, knowing that I would always be on the outside, looking in.

As the rain fell heavier, drumming against the roof above me, I stayed there, motionless, watching her silhouette fade into the distance. Even though she was still so close, she might as well have been on another planet. Her laughter echoed faintly in the humid air, swallowed by the downpour. It was a melody I would never be a part of.

I don't know how long I sat there, staring at nothing, my thoughts circling endlessly around the same empty truth. I had always been invisible to her, but it was only now, after months of holding on to some silent hope, that I had finally accepted it. She was a force of nature—bright, beautiful, untouchable—and I was nothing but a shadow in her world. No matter how often I played out the scenes in my head, imagining her seeing me, acknowledging me, that fantasy would never cross into reality.

I tried to picture what life would be like if I could just let her go. The idea felt foreign like it didn't belong to me. She had become such an integral part of my thoughts, my days, my every quiet moment, that the idea of life without her felt hollow and incomplete. Could I even remember who I was before I fell into this endless longing?

But I had no choice. This obsession, this yearning, was slowly destroying me from the inside. I had spent so much time wrapped up in the idea of her, the possibility of her, that I had lost sight of everything else, my days had been consumed by fleeting moments—a smile she gave someone else, a laugh I overheard, a brief brush of her hand against someone else's arm. I had convinced myself those tiny glimpses were enough to sustain me. But they weren't. They never would be.

As the rain turned into a steady downpour, soaking everything around me, I realized I was stuck. I couldn't move forward. Couldn't go back. I was trapped in this cycle of wanting something I couldn't have. And the worst part? She would never know the damage she had done. She would continue to move through her life, laughing, smiling, completely unaware of the wreckage she left in her wake.

I was nothing more than a distant, fleeting thought if that.

As September crept further in, the days grew shorter, the warmth of summer a distant memory. The sky was often overcast, a thick blanket of grey that seemed to press down on everything, on me. The leaves had just started to change, the green giving way to soft yellows and reds. The streets smelled of wet earth and the beginning of decay, as though the world was preparing to shed its skin for another cycle.

I couldn't shed mine. I carried my feelings like a weight around my neck, dragging me down with every passing day. And yet, even though I knew how much this was hurting me, I couldn't let go. Not yet. Every time I told myself I would try to move on, that I would stop thinking about her, stop letting her consume my thoughts, I'd see her again—laughing, talking, living—and the cycle would start over. The ache in my chest would flare up, burning through me with a sharp intensity that left me breathless.

I had tried to be okay with just watching her, just being a bystander in her life. But now, that felt like a kind of slow torture, an existence where I was forced to endure the constant reminder that I would never matter to her. The more I saw her, the more it hurt, until it felt like every interaction she had with someone else, every smile she gave, was another cut. A thousand little wounds and I was bleeding out without anyone noticing.

September, with its cool breezes and soft rain, became a constant reminder that everything changes—except for me. Except for this.

She still didn't notice me. Not in the way I had once hoped she would. I wasn't even a fixture in her periphery. And yet, she had become the centre of my world, despite not even knowing it. It was a cruel paradox, one I couldn't seem to escape.

And the thing was, I didn't want her to know. Not anymore. I didn't want her pity or her concern. I didn't want to be some sad, broken thing in her life that she felt sorry for. That would be worse than this quiet invisibility. At least this way, I could still pretend that maybe, in some alternate version of this life, she might have seen me differently. That maybe, I would have been enough for her.

But, I was nothing.

The early autumn rain continued, day after day as if the world was washing itself clean. The streets shimmered with moisture, the trees dripped with it, and the air felt thick and heavy like it was on the verge of something. The days blurred together, each one a dull repeat of the last. I tried to fill my time with other things, distractions to keep me from falling deeper into this pit I'd dug for myself, but it was no use. No matter what I did, she was there. In the back of my mind, in the quiet moments, in the spaces between breaths.

I did not know then,but,I was setting myself up for **heartbreak**

CHAPTER SIX

HEART BREAK

October had just begun, and with it came the subtle chill in the air that signalled the arrival of autumn. The school was abuzz with excitement as the Puja holidays approached. Students chattered about their plans—trips to their hometowns, shopping for new clothes, and the pandal-hopping they'd do with friends. The festive spirit spread like wildfire through the hallways and classrooms. But for me, all of it felt distant, like the hum of a song playing from another room. The anticipation that once thrilled me during this time of year was nowhere to be found. Instead, I felt an ache deep in my chest—a heavy, sinking feeling that wouldn't go away.

This year, the festivities were overshadowed by a different kind of anticipation. The farewell of the 2024-25 batch was near, and with it, the end of my last few months with her. Every day that passed brought her closer to leaving. The thought of it was unbearable. I wasn't ready to say goodbye, not when I had never even said what I felt.

The first time I saw her was in the dance room, an unexpected place to encounter someone who would change the way I saw the world. She was with a group of her friends, laughing at something one of them had said. I remember noticing her laugh before anything else—a bright, carefree sound that seemed to echo through the room and reach straight into my heart. Her smile was contagious, and before I knew it, I was smiling too, even though I had no idea what the joke was. From that moment, I was drawn to her in a way I couldn't explain.

The dance room was a place filled with energy and rhythm, but in that moment, everything seemed to slow down. The movement of the dancers blurred into the background, and all I could focus on was her—her laughter, her joy, the way she seemed so alive. It was as if the rest of the world had faded away, leaving just the two of us in that moment. But of course, it wasn't just the two of us. She was surrounded by friends, completely unaware of the impact she had on me.

Before long, I found myself looking for her in the hallways, at lunch, during assemblies. Every glimpse of her felt like a small victory, a moment that I could hold onto and replay in my mind. I never worked up the courage to talk to her, though. What would I even say? That her smile made my day a little brighter. That I couldn't help but feel my heart race every time I saw her. It all sounded so silly, so insignificant in the grand scheme of things. So I kept my distance, content to admire her from afar.

The days passed in a blur, the routine of school life masking the growing anxiety I felt as the end of the year approached. She was always surrounded by friends, always the center of attention, yet she seemed so out of reach. I wondered if she even knew who I was. We had exchanged glances a few times, but that was the extent of our interactions. I was just another face in the crowd to her, another student passing through the halls of a school that she would soon leave behind.

Each day, I would walk through the school with a sense of both anticipation and dread. Anticipation, because I knew I would see her at some point, even if just for a moment. Dread, because I knew that each of those moments was fleeting, slipping away like sand through my fingers. The thought that these brief encounters would soon be gone was almost unbearable.

I tried to focus on my studies, to push thoughts of her to the back of my mind, but it was impossible. Every time I saw her, my heart would skip a beat, and I would be flooded with a mix of emotions—joy at seeing her, and sadness at the thought that she would soon be gone. I spent countless nights lying awake, staring at the ceiling, wondering if I would ever have the chance to tell her how I felt. But the days kept slipping away, and my courage never seemed to grow.

The school felt like a maze, with each hallway and classroom filled with memories of her. I would walk past the dance room, remembering the first time I saw her laugh. I would sit in the canteen, hoping to catch a glimpse of her at her usual table. Even the library, once a place of quiet refuge, became a place of longing as I would catch sight of her through the rows of books.

As the weeks went by, the silence between us became heavier, and more oppressive. It wasn't that we didn't speak because we had nothing to say—it was because there was too much to say, too many words that felt like they would choke me if I tried to voice them. I wanted to tell her everything, to let her know how much she meant to me, but the fear of rejection, of ruining whatever fragile connection we had, kept me silent.

I began to wonder what it would be like to actually talk to her, to have a real conversation instead of just exchanging glances in the hallway. I imagined what her voice would sound like when she spoke directly to me, how her eyes would look when she really saw me, not just as another student, but as someone who cared deeply for her.

But those thoughts were just fantasies, and I knew it. In reality, I was too afraid to take that step, too scared of what might happen if I did. So I continued to watch from afar, my feelings growing stronger with each passing day, but never finding the courage to express them.

When the Puja holidays finally arrived, the school closed for a week, giving everyone a much-needed break from the pressures of exams and assignments. My friends were excited, planning outings and get-togethers, but I couldn't bring myself to care. The thought of spending time away from school, away from her, made the holiday seem more like a punishment than a break.

The festive season, usually a time of joy and celebration, felt hollow to me. I wandered through the bustling streets, watching as people prepared for the festival. Shops were filled with bright clothes, sweets, and decorations, all the colours of the season blending together in a vibrant display of joy. But none of it seemed real to me. My mind was elsewhere, lost in thoughts of her. I wondered what she was doing, if she was with her friends, laughing and enjoying the holiday. I wondered if she ever thought about me, even if just in passing.

Each day of the holiday seemed to drag on endlessly. While everyone around me was caught up in the excitement of the season, I felt disconnected, like I was floating through the days without any real purpose. I missed school—not for the lessons or the routine, but for the chance to see her again. It was strange, this attachment I had to someone who didn't even know me. But it was real, and it was growing stronger with each passing day.

When the holidays ended, I returned to school with a renewed sense of urgency. The farewell was drawing closer, and I knew I didn't have much time left. Every day felt like a countdown, each morning bringing me one step closer to the inevitable goodbye. I started arriving at school earlier, lingering in the hallways where I knew she would pass by, hoping for just a moment to see her, to maybe even exchange a few words.

But as the days went on, I began to realize that I was running out of time. The school was already preparing for the farewell ceremony, with teachers and students working together to make it a memorable event. The seniors were busy with final exams and preparations for the next chapter of their lives, and she was no exception. She seemed more distant than ever, caught up in the whirlwind of exams, college applications, and the excitement of what lay ahead. I could see the anticipation in her eyes, the eagerness to move forward, to leave behind the world of school and step into the future.

And then, one day, I overheard her talking to a friend about her plans after graduation. She spoke with such enthusiasm about the university she had been accepted to, the courses she was excited to take, and the new city she would be moving to. My heart sank as I listened, realizing that she would soon be gone, off to start a new life far away from here, far away from me.

That night, I couldn't sleep. I lay in bed, staring at the ceiling, my mind racing with thoughts of her. I knew I had to do something, to at least try to tell her how I felt before it was too late. So I got out of bed and sat at my desk, pulling out a piece of paper and a pen. The words came slowly at first, but soon they began to flow, pouring out of me like a dam that had finally burst.

I told her everything in that letter—how much she meant to me, how her smile had brightened my days, how I had admired her from afar, too afraid to speak up. I told her that I wished I had been braver, that I had taken the chance to get to know her better. I didn't expect anything from her—I knew that she didn't feel the same way—but I needed her to know how I felt, even if it was too late.

But as the days went on, I couldn't bring myself to give her the letter. What if it made things awkward? What if it ruined the last few days we had left? I didn't want to make things complicated for her, not when she had so much to look forward to. So I kept the letter to myself, carrying it around in my bag, waiting for the right moment that never seemed to come.

The day of the farewell arrived, and the school was transformed. The hallways were decorated with streamers and balloons, and the assembly hall was filled with rows of chairs for the students and teachers. The seniors were dressed in their best, looking more grown-up than I had ever seen them, ready to step out into the world and leave high school behind.

I watched from the sidelines as the ceremony unfolded. There were speeches, performances, and presentations, all celebrating the achievements of the graduating class. She was called up to the stage at one point, receiving an award for academic excellence. I clapped along with everyone else, my heart swelling with pride for her, even though she had no idea how I felt.

As the ceremony drew to a close, the seniors were given a chance to say a few words. She stood up, and I held my breath, hanging on to every word she said. She talked about the memories she had made, the friendships she had formed, and the excitement she felt about the future. But as she spoke, I couldn't help but feel a pang of sadness. She was moving on, ready to embrace the next chapter of her life, and I was being left behind.

After the ceremony, there was a small reception in the school amphitheatre. I watched as she mingled with her friends, laughing and taking pictures, savouring the last moments of her high school life. I knew I had to say goodbye, that this was my last chance to at least wish her well, but my feet felt like they were glued to the ground. I couldn't move, couldn't bring myself to walk up to her and say the words that were stuck in my throat.

The reception ended, and the seniors began to leave, one by one. I watched as she walked towards the gate, her friends by her side, all of them excitedly talking about the future. I wanted to call out to her, to stop her, to give her the letter that was still in my bag, but I couldn't. I just stood there, watching her walk away, feeling the weight of everything I hadn't said pressing down on me.

And then she was gone, disappearing around the corner and out of sight. The last few months had come to an end, and with them, my chance to tell her how I felt. I stood there for a long time, staring at the spot where I had last seen her, the letter still clutched in my hand. The school was empty now, the once lively hallways silent and still. It felt as if the entire world had come to a stop, leaving me alone with my thoughts and regrets.

I walked slowly to the gate, feeling the cool breeze of the evening brushing against my face. The sun was setting, casting a golden hue over the school grounds. It was a beautiful sight, but it felt bittersweet, a reminder that everything was coming to an end.

As I left the school, I couldn't help but think about what could have been. If only I had been braver, if only I had spoken up sooner, maybe things would have been different. But now it was too late, and all I could do was hold onto the memories of the moments we shared, however brief they were.

The days after the farewell were quiet. The school felt empty without the seniors, the hallways quieter, and the classrooms less crowded. Life went on, but there was a void where she used to be, a lingering ache that wouldn't go away. I carried the letter with me for a while, unable to throw it away, but eventually, I knew I had to let go. I took it out one last time, read the words I had written, and then tore it up, letting the pieces scatter in the wind.

It was a strange kind of closure, knowing that I would never see her again, that she had moved on to a new chapter of her life while I remained behind. But there was a small comfort in the fact that she was happy, that she was living the life she had dreamed of. And as for me, I knew I had to move on too, to let go of the past and embrace whatever the future had in store.

But moving on was easier said than done. Everywhere I went, I was reminded of her. The dance room where I first saw her, the cafeteria where she used to sit with her friends, the library where I would catch glimpses of her through the shelves—all of these places were now filled with memories of her, memories that I couldn't escape.

I tried to distract myself, throw myself into my studies and focus on preparing for my own future. But no matter how hard I tried, I couldn't shake the feeling of emptiness that had settled in my chest. I missed her, even though we had never really been close. I missed the way her smile could light up a room, the way her laughter could make even the worst days seem a little brighter.

Years later, as life moved on and the memories of school became distant echoes, I found myself reflecting on that unspoken love. The feelings had long since settled, no longer sharp or overwhelming, but they had never entirely faded. They were a part of me, woven into the fabric of who I had become.

The letter reminded me of the intensity of young love, of how deeply I had felt for her, even though I had never said a word. It was a bittersweet reminder of the person I had been, of the fears and insecurities that had held me back. But it was also a reminder of the capacity for love that I carried within me, a love that, though unfulfilled, had been real and powerful.

As I held the letter in my hands, I realized that those feelings had shaped me in ways I hadn't fully understood until now. They had taught me about the beauty of vulnerability, and about the importance of expressing my emotions, even when it was difficult. And they had shown me that love, even when unspoken, has the power to transform us.

I carefully placed the letter back in the notebook and set it aside. It was no longer a source of regret but a cherished memory—a reminder of a time when love had been all-encompassing, when every glance, every smile, had meant the world to me.

And while life had moved on, and I had moved forward, the memory of that love remained, not as a wound, but as a part of the journey that had led me to where I was. It was a reminder that love, in all its forms, leaves an indelible mark on our hearts, shaping us into the people we are meant to become.

The letter reminded me of the intensity of young love, of how deeply I had felt for her, even though I had never said a word. It was a bittersweet reminder of the person I had been, of the fears and insecurities that had held me back. But it was also a reminder of the capacity for love that I carried within me, a love that, though unfulfilled, had been real and powerful.

The feelings were still there, but they had changed. They were no longer the intense, overwhelming emotions that had consumed me during those final days of school. Instead, they had become something quieter, more peaceful—a sense of fondness and gratitude for the time I had spent with her, even if it had been from a distance.

I have considered keeping the letter, as a memento of that time in my life, but in the end, I decided to let it go. I tore it up, just as I had done before, and watched as the pieces fluttered to the floor. It was a final goodbye, a way of closing that chapter of my life and making room for whatever came next.

Only time will tell what comes next for me but one thing is for sure that school love will go with me to the grave, Even after my **death**

CHAPTER SEVEN

DEATH

"And that was the last time my brother, your uncle, ever wrote something in the diary," said Ved, tears running down his face as he finished narrating the now 20-year-old diary.

"Father, what happened to uncle Shiv after that?" asked his oldest son. His sister, equally curious, leaned in, eager to hear the answer. They had always wondered who their mysterious uncle was and why he was never around. Their father, a doctor and a former coach, always ignored this question. Ved was adept at keeping a straight face in emotional situations, but talking about his brother always made him emotional.

"Well, he... um... After the farewell of the 24-25 batch, he became very silent. As silent as a grave. I never thought that after some years he would be in a grave himself."

The children were visibly shocked and horrified at the sudden revelation. They started to understand the pain he had kept in his heart for such a long time and the reason he became so emotional.

"I never knew that he had become a shell of his former self. He passed classes 11 and 12 with science and even got AIR 18 in NEET. That was the last time I saw him laugh. He was allotted IMS BHU in Banaras. We were shocked that he did not get AIIMS , but we were still happy. At the airport, I saw him alive for the last time. His last hug was so tight, and I later knew why. About a month after he left, I got a letter. At the time, I did not realize it was very weird because he never liked writing letters. But I was so happy to receive it that I did not notice. It said, 'Take care of Mom and Dad, and you can have my bat as my last gift for now. Love, Your Brother.' That letter was the last thing I had from him. Some days after I received the letter, we got the most devastating news I had ever heard. My brother, the role model of my life, had committed suicide by jumping into the Ganges. The worst part is that his body was never recovered." Tears dripped as he finished the sentence.

"When I first heard about my brother's suicide, an overwhelming sense of shock and disbelief washed over me, leaving me paralyzed with grief. The initial moments were a blur of incomprehension and anguish. I struggled to process the magnitude of the loss. Questions swirled in my mind, each one a jagged shard of pain—how could this happen? What could I have done differently? The weight of sorrow was suffocating, and a profound sense of guilt gnawed at my soul. Despite the tumult of emotions, a deep yearning to understand and make sense of the unfathomable tragedy began to take root. But I could not understand why. Why did he kill himself? The man who had helped me win every personal battle, how could he lose to his own mental battle?"

"Dad, how did you cope with losing Uncle?" asked the boy in a cautious tone.

"Well... Losing my elder brother was the most devastating experience of my life. We were not just siblings; we were best friends, confidants, and partners in crime. His absence left a void that nothing could fill.

Memories of our childhood flooded my mind—playing in the backyard, sharing secrets, and supporting each other through thick and thin. He was my role model, my protector, and my mentor. His guidance shaped my worldview, and his laughter was the soundtrack of my life. The pain of his loss was unbearable, and for a long time, I struggled to come to terms with the fact that he was no longer physically present. Each day felt like an uphill battle, and the simple act of getting out of bed became a Herculean task. The world seemed colder, darker, and infinitely lonelier without him by my side. Our bond as siblings was unbreakable. We navigated the rollercoaster of life together, celebrating each other's victories and providing unwavering support during the trials and tribulations. He was the epitome of strength and kindness, and his absence left a palpable void in our family. The dynamics shifted, and the atmosphere at home became sombre. The inside jokes, the late-night conversations, and the shared dreams now only existed in my memories. I often found myself reaching for the phone to share a piece of good news or seek his advice, only to be jolted back to reality by the crushing truth. As time passed, I realized that the best way to honour my brother was to carry forward his legacy. I delved into his passions, embracing his hobbies and interests as my own. In doing so, I felt closer to him, as if a part of his spirit lived on through me. I channelled my grief into action, striving to make a positive impact on his memory. I dedicated myself to causes that were dear to him, finding solace in the knowledge that his values and beliefs continued to thrive through my actions. Keeping his memory alive became my mission, and I found comfort in sharing anecdotes about him with friends and family, keeping the essence of his vibrant personality alive. That is the reason I became a doctor. Losing my elder brother forever altered the fabric of my existence. His absence is a wound that will never fully heal, but it has also been a catalyst for profound personal growth. I carry his legacy with me, drawing strength from his memory and striving to live a life that would make him proud. The pain of his loss remains, but so do the enduring love and cherished memories that continue to shape my journey."

"Dad, why are there so many shayaris in the diary? Was uncle a poet?"

Ved smiled, but his smile showed a hint of anger and a lot of pain. "He became one after meeting the girl he so dearly loved but never confessed to. Now, no more questions. Remember, what is the date tomorrow?"

"It's Uncle's birthday, 26th November."

"Good. Now sleep, or you won't be able to wake up in time to go shopping with me."

"Dad, can I ask you one more thing?"

"What?"

"Did you name me Shivansh to honour your bond with Uncle?"

"Yes," said Ved with tears in his eyes. "Good night now."

Ved switched off the lights and exited the room, holding back tears. He went straight to the bathroom and cried for a while. Then he sat at his office table to write his yearly birthday letter.

"Dear Brother

On this day, as the world celebrates another year of your presence, I find myself grappling with the bittersweet reality of wishing you a happy birthday in your absence. The ache of not being able to embrace you, look you in the eye, and share in the joy of this occasion is a weight that I carry with a heavy heart. Yet, as I sit here, enveloped in memories of your infectious laughter and unwavering love, I am compelled to express the depths of my emotions on this poignant day.

Your birthday was always a time of exuberant celebration, marked by laughter, warmth, and the unmistakable glow of your presence. The joy that emanated from you was infectious, lighting up every corner of the room and infusing the day with an unparalleled sense of merriment. Your ability to make everyone feel cherished and valued remains an indelible part of my recollection, and it is this spirit that I carry with me today.

As I reflect on the countless memories we shared, I am reminded of the profound impact you had on my life and the lives of those around you. Your wisdom, kindness, and unwavering support were beacons of light in even the darkest of times. Your birthday, therefore, becomes a celebration not only of the day you were born but of the beautiful legacy you left behind—a legacy of love, compassion, and boundless generosity.

Though you are no longer physically present, your spirit permeates every facet of my existence. It is in the gentle breeze that rustles through the leaves, in the warmth of the sun's embrace, and in the twinkling of the stars that I sense your enduring presence. Your essence lives on in the memories we created, in the lessons you imparted, and in the love that continues to bind us across the chasm of time and space.

On this day, I find myself overwhelmed with gratitude for the privilege of having shared a part of my life's journey with you. The lessons you taught me, the love you showered upon me, and the indelible mark you left on my heart are cherished beyond measure. Your birthday serves as a poignant reminder to celebrate the precious moments we were blessed to have and to honour the remarkable individual you were.

As I navigate the complexities of life, I am guided by the light of your memory. Your unwavering strength, your unyielding spirit, and your boundless love continue to inspire me to reach for the stars, to embrace empathy and understanding, and live each day with purpose and passion. Your birthday, therefore, becomes a call to action—a call to carry your legacy forward and to embody the values you held dear.

On this day, I find solace in the memories we shared—the laughter that echoed through the halls, the conversations that stretched long into the night, and the unspoken bond that transcended words. Though the ache of your absence lingers, these memories stand as testaments to the enduring power of love and the timeless nature of our connection.

As I send my heartfelt wishes to you on this day, I am enveloped in a tapestry of emotions—love, longing, and an unwavering sense of gratitude for having known you. Though you may no longer be physically present, your birthday remains a day of celebration—a celebration of your life, your love, and the profound impact you had on all who had the privilege of knowing you.

Happy birthday, my dear brother. You are forever cherished, forever missed, and forever loved.

With all my love,

YOUR LONE BROTHER"

As Ved sat at his office table, pouring his heart into the yearly birthday letter to his brother, the weight of the memories and the loss seemed to press down on him with an unbearable heaviness. Each word he wrote was filled with a mix of love, longing, and an overwhelming sense of grief that he had carried for the past twenty years.

His children, now aware of the story behind their uncle, lay in bed with thoughts racing through their minds. They had always sensed a deep sorrow within their father but never truly understood its magnitude until now. The revelation about their uncle's tragic end had left them shaken, but also more empathetic towards their father's pain.

Ved's thoughts drifted back to the days when his brother was alive. He remembered their childhood adventures, the shared dreams, and the unwavering bond that had made them inseparable. The memory of his laughter, his infectious enthusiasm, and his passion for life played in Ved's mind like an old, cherished movie.

The birthday letters had become a tradition, a way for Ved to keep his brother's memory alive and to channel his grief into something meaningful. Each year, as His brother's birthday approached, Ved would sit down and write, allowing himself to relive the moments they had shared, to mourn the future that would never be, and honour the brother he had lost too soon.

As Ved's pen moved across the paper, his tears fell, blurring the ink and smudging the words. But he continued, determined to finish the letter. He wrote about the void that his brother's absence had left in their lives, about the lessons he had learned from his brother, and about how he tried to live up to his legacy.

Exhausted from the emotional toll of writing, Ved fell asleep at his desk, the letter resting beneath his weary head. In his dreams, he was reunited with his brother, and for a brief moment, the pain of the past twenty years faded away, replaced by the warmth of their brotherly bond.

The next morning, Ved's children found him asleep at his desk. They gently woke him up, and Ved, still groggy, smiled at them with a mixture of sadness and love. They knew the day would be difficult, but they were determined to make it a day of remembrance and celebration, just as their father had done for so many years.

Together, they spent the day honouring their uncle's memory, sharing stories, and visiting the places that held special significance to their family. They laughed, they cried, and they found solace in each other, knowing that His brother's spirit lived on through their love and memories.

"Dad can you tell me one thing" Said the son in a very curious tone

Ved in the happiest voice he could use asked "What is it, my son"

"You said uncle was a poet right?"

"Yes, What about it"

"Can you recite his last Sher, Please"

Ved was taken aback by this request, though he still remembered those four lines as clear as day he never expected to recite those to his son

Ved recited the sher, his voice trembling with emotion:

> *""Ab aap dekhenge Rutba hamara*
> *Meri qabra ki ret hai dariya hamara*
> *Kal pitaji keh rahe the kisi se*
> *Mohobbat kha gai Ladka hamara""*

As he spoke the poignant lines, the weight of their meaning hung heavily in the air, enveloping the room in a profound silence. The children, sensing the depth of their father's pain, sat quietly, their curiosity now mixed with a deep sense of empathy and respect.

After a few moments, Ved continued, his voice soft but steady. "Your uncle had a way with words. He poured his heart and soul into his poetry, and these lines were his final gift to us—a glimpse into the turmoil that he battled within. His love, his pain, and his struggles found their way into his verses, and through them, we can still feel his presence."

The children nodded, absorbing every word. They had always known their father as a strong, stoic man, but now they were beginning to see the layers of emotion that lay beneath his composed exterior.

Ved took a deep breath and wiped away a tear. "Your uncle's poetry was his way of coping with his feelings. He found solace in the rhythm of his words and the flow of his thoughts. It's a reminder that sometimes, expressing our emotions can be a lifeline, a way to navigate the storm within."

The children looked at their father with newfound admiration. "Thank you for sharing this with us, Dad," said the son softly.

Ved nodded, his heart swelling with pride and sorrow. "I'm glad you understand. It's important to remember him and honour his memory. Now, let's go shopping and prepare for his birthday celebration. It's a day to remember the good times and the love we shared."

"Father can we see a photo of Uncle"

Without hesitation Ved whipped out his wallet and showed them his brother's last photo

THE LAST PHOTO

They spent the day shopping for flowers, candles, and a small cake—symbols of their love and remembrance. As they walked through the bustling market, Ved shared more stories about his brother, painting a vivid picture of a vibrant, passionate young man whose life had been tragically cut short.

Back at home, they set up a small altar with their uncle's last photograph, surrounded by flowers and candles the atmosphere in the house shifted from sombre to celebratory. It was a testament to their uncles 's enduring spirit and the love that continued to bind their family.

Ved then read aloud a few more of his brother's poems, each one a reflection of his brother's soul and the depth of his emotions. The words resonated deeply with everyone, a reminder of the power of poetry to heal and connect.

As they cut the cake and shared stories, laughter mingled with tears. It was a day of mixed emotions, but through it all, there was a sense of peace and acceptance. They had honoured their uncle's memory in the best way they could—by celebrating his life and cherishing the love that he had left behind.

That night, as Ved tucked his children into bed, he felt a sense of relief. The burden of his grief had been lightened, if only a little, by sharing his brother's story with his children. They had shown him that it was okay to remember, to grieve, and to find solace in each other.

Before turning off the lights, Ved kissed his son's forehead and whispered, "Good night, Shivansh. Thank you for understanding."

As he walked back to his room, Ved felt a renewed sense of purpose. His brother's memory would continue to live on through their stories, their love, and the poetry that had become an integral part of their lives. And as he lay down to sleep, he knew that, in his way, he was keeping his brother's spirit alive, honouring the bond that could never be broken.

At Night, Ved overwhelmed by the day's emotional journey, clung to his wife, finding comfort in her embrace. Her presence was a steady anchor in the turbulent sea of his emotions, and together, they shared the silent understanding of a love forged through shared pain and enduring strength. She also was a school friend and had met his brother he was her favourite senior and was her guide to

"Thank you for being my rock," Ved whispered, his voice breaking. "I couldn't have done this without you."

His wife gently stroked his back, her own eyes filled with tears. "We're in this together, Ved. Always."

That night, as the house settled into quiet, Ved felt a mix of exhaustion and relief. He had finally shared the burden of his brother's memory with his children, allowing them to understand a part of his heart that had been shrouded in silence for so long. The process was painful, but it also brought a profound sense of healing.

As he lay in bed, Ved's thoughts drifted back to his brother's poetry. Those verses etched deeply into his soul, were more than just words; they were a testament to Shiv's inner world, his struggles, and his silent cries for help. The last sher, in particular, reverberated in Ved's mind, a haunting reminder of the pain Shiv carried.

> "*"Ab aap dekhenge Rutba hamara*
> *Meri qabra ki ret hai dariya hamara*
> *Kal pitaji keh rahe the kisi se*
> *Mohobbat kha gai Ladka hamara"*"

Ved closed his eyes, letting the weight of those words wash over him. Shiv's poetry had always been a window into his soul, and even now, it served as a bridge connecting Ved to his lost brother. Through the poetry, Ved could almost hear Shiv's voice, feel his presence, and share in the profound bond they once had.

The next morning, Ved awoke with a renewed sense of determination. Today would be different. It would be a day of his kids knowing their uncle and his life

"Happy birthday, brother," Ved whispered, his voice filled with love and sorrow.

The children, sensing the solemnity of the moment, stood quietly, each lost in their thoughts. They had come to understand the depth of their father's grief and the significance of this day. It wasn't just about mourning a loss;

it was about celebrating a life that had touched theirs in ways they were only beginning to comprehend.

After the moment of silence, Ved suggested they share their favorite memories of Shiv. One by one, they recounted stories they had heard from Ved over the years—tales of youthful adventures, acts of kindness, and moments of laughter that defined Shiv's spirit.

As they spoke, the atmosphere lightened. Laughter mingled with tears, and the room was filled with a palpable sense of love and remembrance. Ved's heart swelled with pride and gratitude. His children were embracing Shiv's memory, finding joy in the stories and drawing strength from the legacy he had left behind.

Before bed, Ved and his wife sat together, reflecting on the day. "I think Shiv would be proud of us," Ved said softly. "We've found a way to honour him and keep his spirit alive."

His wife nodded, her eyes filled with warmth. "He would be. And I'm proud of you, Ved. You've shown incredible strength today, Well, I just have one question"

"What is it"Ved asked curiously

"What was the name of the girl your brother loved so dearly?"

"I tried to ask him many times, but he only answered with the same poem over and over, so I just decided to give up" replied Ved with a casual yet sorrowful voice

"Well what was the poem" asked his wife with an excited face

"well"

"Shayar hoon
Hakim nahi
Rota hoon

EK-EK ko rulata nahi
Ek itihaas ka hissa hoon
Launga ek sitara kabhi
Ek ladki ke piche pagal zarur hoon
Kabhi uska naam bataunga sahi
Haaste rahonge tum
Aur angaro sa jalta jaunga main har ghadi"

As they lay down to sleep, Ved felt a sense of peace he hadn't known in years. The burden of his grief had been lightened, not just by sharing Shiv's story, but by witnessing the love and understanding that his children had shown. They were a testament to the enduring bond of family and the power of memory to heal and connect.

In the quiet of the night, Ved whispered a final goodnight to his brother, knowing that Shiv's spirit would always be a part of their lives. The love they shared, the memories they cherished, and the poetry that spoke of Shiv's soul would continue to guide them, reminding them of the strength found in togetherness and the enduring power of love.

Epilogue

Years passed, and the memory of Shiv lived on in Ved's family, like a quiet yet persistent flame. His poetry became a source of comfort for Shivansh and his sister, Ayesha, as they grew older—a reminder of the uncle they had never met but whose life had shaped theirs in ways they couldn't fully comprehend. They often gathered to read his poems together, finding solace in the verses that had once been his silent cries for help and now served as a bridge to their own emotions.

The poetry wasn't just a pastime; it was a ritual of healing. In the silence of their home, Shiv's words echoed, weaving threads of connection between the past and present. As Shivansh grew into a man, he often found himself wondering what his uncle's voice might have sounded like, how it would have felt to have him there, sharing wisdom, laughing at jokes. He asked his father about it once, during one of their late-night conversations.

"Baba," Shivansh had said, his voice soft in the dim light of the living room, "Do you think Uncle Shiv knew... like, really knew how much you loved him?"

Ved had looked up from the book he was reading, his eyes soft with a mixture of surprise and understanding. He closed the book slowly, resting it on his lap. "I don't know," he admitted after a moment. "I tried. I hope he did. But there's always that doubt, you know? Whether you've said enough, done enough. Whether you were there when they needed you most."

Shivansh nodded, chewing on his lower lip thoughtfully. "It's just... when I read his poems, it feels like he was so alone. Like he thought no one was listening."

Ved's heart clenched at that. It was something he had wrestled with for years—the guilt of not seeing, not understanding, not acting soon enough. But in his years of reflection, in his work as both a doctor and an advocate, he had come to terms with one truth: "People can love you more than anything in the world, and you can still feel alone. It's... not something love can always fix. But I think, in his own way, Shiv knew we cared. Maybe not in the way he needed us to, but I believe he knew."

Ved's own journey with his brother's memory was a long and winding one. After Shiv's death, the grief had consumed him, overwhelming him with questions that had no answers. Why hadn't he seen the signs? Why hadn't Shiv said anything, asked for help? It was a heavy burden to carry, one that he wore like a second skin. But as the years passed, Ved began to channel that grief into something larger than himself—something that honored his brother in a way that Shiv might have understood if he were still alive.

The foundation Ved established in Shiv's name was born out of this need to do something, to create meaning out of tragedy. Named The Shiv Stotra Foundation, it became a beacon of hope for young people struggling with mental health issues, especially in academic settings. Ved worked closely with schools, universities, and mental health professionals, creating programs that offered support to students who, like Shiv, felt lost in the pressure to succeed. His wife—who had once known Shiv as her senior and mentor—became an integral part of the foundation. Together, they spearheaded campaigns, organized seminars, and held workshops, determined to prevent others from slipping through the cracks.

Shivansh, inspired by his uncle's life and his father's dedication, pursued a career in literature. He became a well-known poet, often citing his uncle as his greatest influence. His first book of poetry, titled The Lost Sher, was a tribute to Shiv—a collection of poems written in the style that his uncle had perfected. It became a bestseller, resonating with readers who found pieces of their own struggles within its pages. Shivansh's poetry, much like his uncle's, was raw and honest, a reflection of the emotions he had inherited from a man he never met but whose legacy had shaped him in profound ways.

Every year, on Shiv's birthday, Ved stood in front of a crowd, sharing his brother's story. He didn't sugarcoat the pain or the loss, but he also didn't let it define the narrative. Shiv had been more than his suffering. He had been brilliant, compassionate, full of life. "My brother," Ved would say, "was a poet. He had a way with words that could make you feel things you didn't even know you were carrying. His life wasn't perfect, and it wasn't easy, but it mattered. It still matters."

And at the end of every speech, Ved would recite Shiv's last sher, his voice steady yet laden with emotion. The audience always fell silent, hanging on to the weight of each word, as if Shiv himself were there, speaking through his brother.

One day, years after the foundation had been well-established, Ved and his family gathered for one of their yearly rituals: reading through Shiv's old notebooks. It was a tradition they had started shortly after his passing, a way to keep him close even in death. They never knew what they would find in the faded pages of his journals—sometimes poems, sometimes half-finished thoughts, and sometimes just fragments of a mind that had been in turmoil.

As Shivansh leafed through one of the notebooks, something caught his eye. Tucked between the pages of a well-worn journal was a letter, written in Shiv's handwriting but never addressed. It was creased and yellowed with age, as if it had been folded and unfolded many times. Shivansh's heart raced as he gently pulled it out and handed it to his father.

Ved's hands shook slightly as he opened the letter, his eyes scanning the familiar script. It was dated just a few months before Shiv's death, and the words, though brief, hit Ved like a tidal wave.

> "*Dear Ved,*
> *I don't know if I'll ever give this to you. Maybe I will, maybe I won't. But I just want you to know, I'm proud of you. I'm sorry if I haven't said that enough, or if I haven't been the best brother. You're doing amazing things. I know you'll go on to do even more. I'm just... tired, I guess. But it's not your fault. It's no one's fault. You're a good brother. I love you.*
> *Shiv.*"

The room fell silent as Ved read the letter aloud, his voice thick with emotion. He paused at the end, his eyes brimming with tears, but there was a peace in his heart that hadn't been there before. It wasn't closure—not entirely—but it was something close to it. Shiv had known, after all. He had known how much Ved loved him, how much he mattered.

Shivansh reached out and placed a hand on his father's shoulder, offering a quiet, steadying presence. "He knew, Baba," he whispered. "He really knew."

Over the years, Shivansh and Ayesha grew into adults, each carrying their uncle's legacy in their own way. Ayesha, with her empathetic heart and keen intellect, pursued a career in psychology, inspired by her family's work with mental health advocacy. She often volunteered with the foundation, counseling students who were struggling with their own mental health challenges. She had a way of making people feel seen, heard, and understood—qualities that reminded Ved of his late brother.

Shivansh, on the other hand, followed in Shiv's footsteps, becoming a poet. His love for literature had always been there, nurtured by the countless hours spent reading his uncle's work. But as he grew older, it became more than just a hobby—it became a calling. He often cited Shiv as his greatest influence, and his first book of poetry, The Lost Sher, was a tribute to the uncle he had never met but whose words had shaped his life. The book was a collection of poems written in the style that Shiv had perfected—raw, honest, and deeply personal. It became a bestseller, resonating with readers who found pieces of their own struggles within its pages.

For Ved, watching his children carry forward Shiv's legacy was both a source of pride and a bittersweet reminder of what could have been. But there was peace in knowing that Shiv's story hadn't ended in tragedy. His brother's memory had sparked something beautiful—a movement, a legacy that would continue long after he was gone. Shiv's words, once whispered in the darkness of his pain, now brought light to others.

But it wasn't always easy. There were still moments when the weight of Shiv's absence hit Ved unexpectedly—like when he would hear a song on the radio that reminded him of their childhood, or when he came across an old photograph of the two of them laughing together, arms slung over each other's shoulders. The grief never fully disappeared; it simply evolved, becoming a quieter presence in his life, something he carried with him always.

In the quiet of his study, Ved often found himself writing letters to Shiv. It was something he had started doing a few years after Shiv's death—a way to stay connected, even if the letters would never be read. He wrote about everything: the foundation, his children, the small moments of joy and the bigger challenges that life threw his way. And every year, on Shiv's birthday, he wrote a special letter—a letter filled with love, gratitude, and a deep sense of connection that transcended the boundaries of life and death.

On one such birthday, as Ved sat at his desk, pen in hand, he found himself reflecting on how much had changed since that fateful day when Shiv's life had been cut short. The pain was still there, but it had transformed into something deeper, something that held space for both sorrow and hope.

"Dear Shiv"

He wrote, the familiar ache settling in his chest as he began,

> *"It's your birthday today. Another year without you. And yet, I feel like you've been with me every step of the way. It's funny, isn't it? How someone can be gone and still feel so present?"*

He paused, staring out the window as the late afternoon sun cast a golden glow over the garden.

"Shivansh has become quite the poet, you know. You'd be so proud of him. He reminds me of you in so many ways—his passion, his intensity. Ayesha is doing amazing work too. She's helping so many people, just like you wanted to. They carry you with them, just like I do. We all do."

Ved swallowed, his throat tightening as he continued.

"I don't ask 'why' anymore. I used to, but I've come to understand that some questions don't have answers. And maybe that's okay. Maybe it's enough to just say thank you. Thank you for being with me all these years, brother. Thank you for everything you gave me, even when you didn't know you were giving it. I carry you with me always."

And so, every year, on the 26th of November, Ved and his family gathered to celebrate Shiv's life. They lit candles, shared stories, and read aloud his poetry. The pain of his loss remained, but it had transformed into something deeper—an enduring reminder that love, even in its most painful forms, could transcend time, space, and even death itself.

The quiet flame of Shiv's memory burned on, steady and eternal. His words—once lost in the silence of his suffering—had found their way into the hearts of those who needed them most. In them, he lived on, not as a ghost of tragedy, but as a beacon of hope, resilience, and love.

Htv Lmob R Xlgow Mlh Svmw

Sn

Sgd fhqk H knud

H mdudq gnodc sn bnmptdq xntq knud, H itrs vzmsdc
sn ad sgdqd

ad sgdqd sn lzjd t gzoox, sgdqd vdqd shldr sgzs H sgntfgs H
rgntkc bnmedrr zmc ad sgd adrs xnt gzud dudq rddm

Sgd Rgzxzq rshkk qduhudr sgd knud H edks zmc xnt jmnv
H knud xnt RGQDDKDJGZ

KNUD

About The Author

Siddhanth Rawat is a young, emerging writer and a school student with a natural talent for storytelling. With a deep interest in human emotions and personal experiences, he took a bold step in sharing his thoughts and feelings with the world through his debut book, 7 Stages of One-Sided Love.

This first book explores the intricacies of unreciprocated affection, a theme that resonates deeply with many readers, especially those navigating the challenges of youth and self-discovery. Written from the perspective of someone experiencing these emotions firsthand, Siddhanth brings authenticity and heartfelt sincerity to the pages, capturing the universal feelings of longing, hope, and personal growth.

Aside from writing, he is an avid Poet, always finding new ways to channel creativity. Whether through music, art, or spending time with friends, Siddhanth draws inspiration from everyday life, transforming real-world experiences into powerful, relatable narratives.

As a student, he balances academics with creative pursuits, always driven by a passion to understand the world and connect with others through the written word. Siddhanth is committed to continuing his writing journey, with plans to explore more themes of love, identity, and growth in future works.

www.ingramcontent.com/pod-product-compliance
Lightning Source LLC
Chambersburg PA
CBHW020604160726
47991CB00002B/864